Only If

Only If

Only If

Change Your Life, Live Your Dream

© 2014 Linda Lee Pope

All Rights Reserved. The author grants no assignable permission to reproduce for resale or redistribution. This license is limited to the individual purchaser and does not extend to others. Permission to reproduce these materials for any other purpose must be obtained in writing from the publisher except for the use of brief quotations within book chapters.

Disclaimer
All rights reserved. No part of this book may be used or reproduced by any means, graphic, scanning, electronic, or mechanical, including photocopying, recording, taping or by any information storage retrieval system without the written permission of the publisher except in the case of brief quotations embodied in critical articles and reviews.

ISBN: 978-1-942731-04-7

Published by M&B Global Solutions Inc.
United States of America (USA)

Only If

Change Your Life, Live Your Dream

Linda Lee Pope

Only If

Dedication

To Joyce, my confidant, soul mate, mentor and dear friend.
You taught me what the "warm and fuzzy" feeling was.
We explored "letting go and letting God," and unconditional love.
Without our letters since 1997, my growth and this book would never be.

Only If

Contents

Introduction	9
Paradise or Paradise Realized	11
The Early Years - Finding My Dream	17
Becoming a Woman	33
Changing My Thoughts, Changing My Life	45
The Decision	65
On The Market	75
The Reunion of Survivors	83
The Estate Sale	95
Letting Go and Saying Goodbye	105
September 11, 2001	111
Falling Into Place	125
Five Days To Closing	135
The Sendoff	143
Epilogue	149
Resources	152
Acknowledgements	154
About the Author	157

Only If

Only If

Introduction

We all have pivotal moments or years in our lives. I seem to have several turning points in mine. These were moments calling out for change. These were opportunities to stumble and fall or rise above it all – to learn and grow. Sometimes I learned my lessons right away. Sometimes I needed repeat performances to get the message.

Somehow I managed to get through all these experiences, and their lessons have brought me to the woman I am today. I spent my first five and a half years raised in the tiny city of Goodman, Wisconsin, by my grandmother, then back to live with my parents in 1950. The death of my mother in 1959, my divorce, the death of my brother in 1977, and the death of my daughter in 1984 all were devastating.

The one bright light in all the darkness was a trip to Maui in 1986. I had a special experience at the Sacred Pools of Ohei'o. I was seated on a huge boulder at the end of twenty-two small waterfalls cascading from the 10,023-foot elevation of the dormant Haleakala volcano. I was within twenty feet of the Pacific Ocean. It was an experience that helped me re-shape my life.

The purchase of a business and home within five days of each other in 1987 would seem to be high point in one's life, but a business and home come with their own set of challenges: employees to manage, sales to create

Only If

and maintain, and a home requiring decorating and upkeep; all by me, a single parent. Yet lessons come with life experiences.

I came to realize my entire life had been filled with a succession of stumbling blocks or stepping stones, choices and decisions, challenges and changes. My life changed daily. It was now time for me to take charge of the changes.

By the time March 19, 2001, rolled along, I had a sneaking suspicion 2001 was going to be a year to be remembered. This year would be the most pivotal year of them all. This time I was in complete control. I made the choices. I met the challenges. I changed. Or had I really been changing all along?

This is my journey from my birth in 1945 to landing on Maui On October 30, 2001. I had a few bumps along the road that were opportunities to change my thoughts, change my life, learn and grow.

Thanks for coming along for the ride. Enjoy.

Linda Lee Pope
June 30, 2014

Only If

Paradise or Paradise Realized

It is almost 10 a.m. on a beautiful Saturday morning. I am snuggled into a bamboo swivel rocker with my feet on a footstool. My last cup of coffee for the morning is on the side table. I do the majority of my writing on my computer, but today I am jotting my thoughts on a legal pad as I gaze out the window.

I live in a rented 520-square-foot cottage. I have a good-sized bedroom and a small office in the second bedroom. I have an "efficiency" kitchen with just 36 inches of counter space. If I would lay the refrigerator on its side, there would only be about two feet to get to the kitchen door. There is a little dining counter with two stools facing west. It is small, but so comfy.

My little "great room" has a cathedral ceiling. There are dark brown 4 x 4 beams against an aged, dark brown plank ceiling. There is a west-facing picture window and north-facing sliding glass door, each with cream-colored vertical blinds. I made a 14-inch, bright red valance to top off each window – red is my color, after all. There is just enough room in here for a 72-inch round glass-top table with a bamboo base, and three of the four matching bamboo chairs. I recovered the seat and back cushions in a bright red fabric print with white hibiscus and pale yellow throats. On the glass table is a 24-inch black wrought iron candleholder with an open and curved base. On top is a red candle, with red and white artificial flowers entwining the base, spilling across the glass tabletop.

There is a matching bamboo end table that holds my tall arrangement of white orchids and cascades of red tea roses. I have a fern on top of the television set and another on top of the kitchen cabinet holding the service counter. White flowers cascade from the top of the kitchen cabinet.

The sliding glass door opens to the carport I cross to get to my deck. On the north side of the deck is a Mock Orange bush. Back in Wisconsin, we would see a 12-inch plant over the winter holidays. This "plant" is about 25 feet long and a good 20 feet tall. The Mock Orange is approaching the end of its current bloom. There is the usual 15 to 25 mph trade wind blowing here today, and my home is engulfed in the sweet and heady fragrance of the Mock Orange blossoms. Just now I am watching a "snowfall" of spent flower petals being blown from the bush, covering my deck and furniture in drifts of fragrant white.

My deck has a water fountain display I put together from this and that, and a gift card from my sister, Lisa. I have a white plastic table with two chairs. There are cushions and pads I put out when I use the deck. There are two lounge chairs as well – just waiting for company. True to my goal, I have container gardens. One holds my basil and trailing red nastrums. I keep two impatiens under the dining table to protect them from the hot afternoon sun. One is white and the other looks like tiny roses and is white with a purple frill in the very tip.

I have a ruby red mandevilla vine that has climbed up nine feet of the vertical support beam and has continued nine feet along the cross beam. Not knowing where to grow next, the vines have just grown out to the air and are now dangling down from the beam. They are adorned with many ruby red flowers that dance in the breeze of the trade winds.

On the northwest end of the deck is a pot with a Roma tomato plant doing quite nicely. I have a small, rectangular planter filled with six plugs of mixed lettuce greens. And there is a large tub containing two bags of soil and other additives that have already grown green beans, basil and assorted flowers. Right now, there are hot pink New Guinea impatiens. Flowers do well in winter here, but green beans do better from March to October.

Twice this morning I have noticed my pair of cardinals whizzing past my window. There are the usual sparrows chirping away and a few "rice birds" that feed on the flowers of the Red Bottle Brush tree. There are Franklins, a quail-like bird, that scamper in coves across the small pasture below my deck. A variety of doves I have yet to learn the names of call to one another from tree to tree and to the valley below. They are not like the mourning doves I have known for fifty-seven years, but doves all the same.

I daily hear the call of pheasants on the other side of the pasture. Almost every time I leave my home, there are male and female pheasants walking along or flying over the road. And there are the ever-present common myna birds – akin to the crows of the Midwest – calling as they soar on the thermal.

I see six sheep in the pastureland on a daily basis. They are always grazing with twenty-eight and more goats, as their kids nurse and frolic in the field. There are several varieties of chickens. Thankfully, they usually stay at their home in the early mornings, so I don't often hear the cocks crowing a dawn. And last but not least are two strange female geese, who are convinced they are the rulers of the property. They try to maintain that status daily as they cackle and chase a kid, or the ram or sheep ever so often. Yes, I do live in the country. The landlord and landlady are very kind and thoughtful people, and lovingly call this place the "funny farm." Just my kind of place.

From my living room and deck I can see the south shore of Maui and the communities of Wailea and Kihei. A little further along the shore is Ma'alae Harbor. I can see out to McGregor Point, and then the road goes around the mountain to Lahaina and Kaanapali. A little further out to the southwest is the island of Lanai. Due south is the island of Kaho'okawe and an ancient caldaria called Molokini, known for snorkeling, scuba diving, and its coral reef and green turtle wildlife preserve.

The Island of Hawaii, called the Big Island by locals, is further to the southeast. Since the volcano started erupting in 1983, it is rare to see Hawaii from here, but it does happen on occasion. Once I start down the mountain on Kula Highway, I can see a little part of Molokai hidden by the West Maui Mountains.

Directly across from me is a range of mountains, a dormant volcano that is 1.5 million years old and tops out at just over five thousand feet. It rains almost daily in those ancient valleys and crevasses eroded over the millennia. There is a tropical rainforest with those valleys. Filling the valley between the West Maui Mountains and me is a patchwork quilt made from stands of trees, brush, and sugar cane fields and pineapple fields.

To the north end of the valley, nestled in the foothills of Iao Valley, is the county seat of Wailuku with all the major county, state and federal buildings. Wailuku is the oldest community here. Just down the road from Wailuku is Kahului, settled right on the north shore. It is our largest community and has the airport, Costco, Walmart, Kmart, Lowe's and Home Depot, several malls of all sizes, and just about every service business, restaurant, retail store, and adventure travel activities business one could ask for.

To the north are the shores that welcome the big swells of the winter. The shores attract people from all over the world for the experience of surfing the big waves on a board or with a sail attached to a surfboard, called windsurfing. The Pacific Ocean surrounds me and carries the waves that can build to twenty to forty feet from winter storm swells in the Sea of Japan and the Aleutian Islands. I live 20 degrees above the equator, 2,500 feet above sea level, on the west side of Haleakala. This is an agricultural area called Up Country by the locals.

It is November 16, 2002, and I am experiencing year two, day one, of the fulfillment of a forty-year dream of living on a tropical island. On a cold and blustery October 30, 2001, I boarded a plane in Green Bay, Wisconsin. Just fifteen days earlier I had closed on the sale of my fourteen-year-old, 1,080-square-foot home. I either sold or gave away ninety-nine percent of my material possessions.

I landed on Maui, Hawaii, about 7 p.m. The sun had set more than an hour earlier. A light shower had refreshed the valley only an hour before my arrival, leaving behind the fragrance of an earth renewed and the scents of the tropical flowers riding on the tropical breeze of a balmy 82-degree evening.

The rising "blue moon" of October lay low in the black sky as I drove to Makawao and my rented room. A multitude of twinkling stars filled out the background of the gigantic silver moon, backlighting the top of Haleakala. Haleakala – The House of the Rising Sun – was wearing her necklace of thousands of twinkling lights I would come to know lights of Makawao, Pukalani and my beloved Kula – Up Country.

Only If

    This last paragraph was my first hour on Maui. This has been my story from my birth in 1945 to my decision to move to Hawaii in 2001 to my dream fulfillment. How I made my **dream** become my **reality**.

    What is your dream and how will you make your dream come true?

Only If

The Early Years – Finding My Dream

I was born in 1945 in Baraboo, Wisconsin. My parents were married in 1944 and worked at the Badger Ammunitions plant. The plant made powder and bombs to replenish supplies depleted in the Second World War. Married couples were fine, but no children were allowed. When I came along, they were faced with losing their jobs or finding a place for me to be.

My mom gave me to my grandparents to raise until the demand for ammunition was filled. My Aunt Sadie told me this story when I was forty-five years old. She said my mom thought Grandma did a good job raising her kids and that all turned out good.

Badger Ammunitions was the largest plant of its kind in the USA and continued production on various products for the Korean and Vietnam wars and other conflicts until 1975. As fate would have it, Mom became pregnant with Leeanna's birth expected in 1950, and they decided to make a home for their soon-to-be family of four in Cottage Grove, Wisconsin, near Madison.

I spent my entire first five and one-half years living with my grandparents and five other family members in their home, including Aunt Joan, who had moved back home because her husband, Loren, was stationed in Europe. I remember the day Loren returned home to claim his wife. There was a banging at the front door. This giant of a man was standing there with this huge duffle bag at his feet. I called upstairs for Joan and she came bounding down the stairs screaming his name until they were in each other's arms.

We would pile in cars and go to Hilbert Lake for family reunions, picnics and swimming. The transplanted families from Madison and Manitowoc, Wisconsin, would make the trip with trailers and tents to camp out at the lake or yards in Goodman. But the nights before the big day were always the best. Big washtubs were used to make two kinds of potato salad. Grandma baked all the breads and buns every day anyway, so triple batches were not a problem. A master menu was made and people chose what to bring. We had a family of great cooks, but it was the joking and banter that was the best part.

I loved the chaos, the dancing, listening to the radio and Victrola playing large 78-speed records. There were Help Thy Neighbor and Michigan Rummy games to play. Grandma would bring out her coffee can of pennies and be the banker. She won a lot of the pots and needed a second coffee can as well.

There was fishing in town at Clark Lake and collecting wild raspberries when we were done. Not all of the berries made it home. When the family was much younger, I was told my grandparents would take their family into the woods to fish for trout. They would make a fire and cook the fish. On the way home, they would pick wild blueberries that made a mighty fine dessert. In later years, my grandfather became a fishing guide for the local Coleman Fishing Club.

I used to love to sit on her big front porch and talk to my grandmother. She was so kind and wise. We would rock back and forth in her porch swing, sometimes taking the two afghans to stave off the chill of the day or at dusk. People would pass by in cars or on the sidewalk, and everyone greeted her with Mrs. Millette, Grandma Millette or Grandma Helen. She was everyone's mother. She may have had nine kids, but everyone would bring a friend or two home for lunch or after-school snacks. So now you know why she had to bake every day!

Every time there was a football game at the high school across the street, my grandma would attend. During halftime, family and friends would fill her kitchen for chili or soups, or cold cuts and sweets. Then it was back to the high school for the end of the game, and then back to Grandma's for a victory party.

Their home was filled with love and sharing, kindness and thoughtfulness, respect and love. When you did wrong, you were disciplined and then loved. Hugs, kisses, and going to church was the ritual of the Millettes. Yes, Grandma did a good job raising her family, and so I was given to my grandparents to be raised. They were gifts my mom gave to me.

I left all this behind – my grandparents, aunts and uncles – to move to Cottage Grove with something called "parents," who I did not know. I just wanted to return to my grandparents.

I started first grade in August and my sister, Leeanna, was born in October. I remember her crawling around getting stuck behind the sofa or lost in the closet that had material for a door. You couldn't have a conversation with her, play games, dance or run outside with her. I missed the big kids I used to play with. I missed the hugs, kisses, sitting on someone's lap and being read to. I was forty-five before I knew the story of my grandparents raising me and finally understood that my grandparents did not send me away, but rather gave me back to my parents.

Only If

The year is now 1959. Gas is about 25 cents – that is twenty-five cents a gallon! Drive-in theaters and drive-in eating places are very popular. McDonald's had been around for a few years in Madison, Wisconsin. For three dollars you could get ten hamburgers, ten bags of fries and ten drinks! You could buy three pounds of freshly ground hamburger for a dollar. My mom and dad spent six dollars on a new dress for me because I was about to graduate from eighth grade at Badger Elementary School and go on to ninth grade in Central High School in downtown Madison.

I was a very naive thirteen-year-old when I had the well-known "Mother-Daughter Tea." Yes, it was my introduction to the curiosities of feminine hygiene, the female body and the reproductive system. I learned a little bit more than I wanted to know at the time, let me tell you. You get what? You do what?

I loved to listen to 45-rpm records. I loved the radio and listening to the big band music I used to dance to with my aunts and uncles years before. My favorites were the Benny Goodman and Glenn Miller bands, along with singers like Doris Day, the Andrews Sisters and Judy Garland, who sang songs of the day from the 1940s and early 1950s. Hank Williams, Vaughn Monroe, Eddy Arnold and Bing Crosby had crossover hits from country to contemporary music.

The late 1950s were a time for the music to change along with this generation. I sang along and danced, pretending to be a movie star, recording artist, or Broadway star performing to my admiring fans. We got "All Shook Up" with a "Whole Lot of Shaking Going On" while we were "At The Hop!" In a romantic mood, I knew "To Know Him is To Love Him," but I knew "It Was Only Make Believe" as Pat Boone sang about our "Love Letters In The Sand." And then there was Ricky Nelson and his family on television.

Only If

I was happy and free of cares. I took long walks on the nine acres of land that came with the large three-bedroom home we rented. There were wild raspberries and loganberries galore. There were apple and pear trees, and plenty of cleared land for a garden that provided jars and jars of canned goods to fill our tummies for the next year. There were always two 20-gallon crocks of pickles – one to feast on over the summer and one for my mother to "put up" for the winter.

We picked young dandelion greens to eat in place of spinach that was not yet ready–and believe me, I knew the difference! We collected the young, tender flower buds that my dad and mom used to make into one crock of dandelion wine (icky) each year. Then the last crock was used for my mother to make sauerkraut–a must for my mom's German and French-Canadian heritages. Then my favorite, two crocks of dill pickles. It all seemed so idyllic.

But then in life, things change. There was a big hurt in May with the death of my favorite aunt, Marcella. She was twice my age, but was my best friend and my mother's 26-year-old sister.

I remember many fun experiences with my aunt in her north woods hometown of Goodman, Wisconsin. From toasting potato chips with a cigarette lighter, to standing as a lookout while my aunts and uncles (teenagers) were "reconnoitering" green apples from someone else's apple trees, to using wax paper to wiz down the metal slide fire escape at the high school across the street from my grandmother's home, we found ways to have fun

We had smudge pots on summer evenings to stave off the mosquitoes as we played Statues and Run Sheep Run. Just before the 9 p.m. curfew, Grandpa Millette would put out the fire. We would watch the glowing embers float off into the black of the night and disappear. Grandpa or one of the boys would remove the stones from the galvanized smudge pot and there would be the most perfectly roasted and toasted potatoes for all of us to enjoy.

Grandma Millette called my aunt Marcella Mae – especially when she was in trouble yet again. I just called her Marcie. Marcie managed to live more than twice as long as the doctors had predicted. In 1933, she had been born with most of her vital organs outside her body. Many surgeries solved the problems over the first few years of her life. Everyone was amazed that she lived at all, but she lived her life to the fullest. She married in 1952 and had a good seven years of marriage, adopting a baby girl as well. She finally succumbed to kidney disease on May 10, 1959.

I remember my dad waking me up in the middle of a raging spring thunderstorm. This was not at all strange for Mom and Dad to wake me up so we could watch the thunder and lightning on our huge screened-in porch. Occurrences of nature at its strongest were best experienced with my siblings, accompanied by mom's salted and buttered popcorn served in brown shopping bags.

My dad would make lemonade from packaged or fresh lemons, but always served with slivers of lemon in glasses filled with ice. We would park ourselves at the big, old claw-foot oak table on the porch and watch the storms. Thunderstorms were something to be honored, but never feared. We were made mindful of the dangers of a storm and learned to respect them. We also absorbed their beauty and majesty.

But this wake-up call from my dad was not as I had thought. Dad told me to me to go downstairs and try to comfort my mom. She had just heard of her sister's death and he wanted my help.

Only If

I could see my mother sitting in the parlor on our maroon camelback sofa. I could see the slender shape of my mother's body silhouetted against sheer curtains as the flashes of lightening lit the parlor and the sky, followed by another boom of thunder and strike of lightening. I just wanted to become part of the rosebud wallpaper and disappear.

My mom sat with her knees drawn up to her chin, clutching her legs, her chestnut-colored hair moving with the shaking of her body as she trembled and cried her heart out. I was in so much pain and so was she. I had no words at thirteen and could do nothing to comfort my mother but cry with her, for us to hold each other and be together to ease her pain.

The loss of Marcie was so quick. I was never told of her health issues so I had no expectations of death – why would you for someone twenty-six? She was living far away in Texas, where Uncle Pete was stationed. There was no time to say goodbye. I would never see her again. It was all so confusing. What do I do now?

Somehow I made it through Marcie's death, the "tea," and my eighth grade graduation. This would be my last summer as a "kid," that was for sure. In the fall I would be going to high school, fourteen, and in ninth grade. I would be a real teenager and not a child any longer. Yes, I had great plans for this summer. There were long walks to take, many books to be read, and records to listen to and songs to sing.

Unfortunately, my parents had plans for me as well. And so my June, July, and half of August were filled with their plans, which included lawn mowing, babysitting my brother and three sisters, and helping in the huge garden. Weeding, picking, and watching the kids as Mom and Dad worked in the garden, and canning.

Only If

On July 24, 1959, Mom had my sister, Lisa. The family grew to six kids now, but we were not in any want or need. The garden and orchards provided all the fresh and canned fruits and vegetables one could want. Pickles, juices, vegetables and even canned meats lined the shelves. Dad had been working at Oscar Meyer for about ten years. It paid well and there was always any kind of beef, pork or poultry product one could buy.

But life took a change once again. On August 16, just three weeks after Lisa was born, my mom died as a result of an auto accident within a mile from our home. We lived half a block from the West Beltline Highway around Madison, and I remember hearing all the police sirens and wondering what had happened.

Our family's pink Chevrolet Bel Air was crossing a four-lane divided boulevard on Park Street. There was a city bus a couple of blocks away approaching the intersection on the inside lane. Dad thought it was safe to cross Park Street from the center section, but he was wrong. There was a speeding car on the other side of the bus. They could not see my dad, and my dad could not see them.

The unstoppable high-speed impact happened. The car hit the passenger side straight on and mom was thrown from the car and received massive injuries. She died on the operating table about four hours after the accident. The only comfort I could find was in knowing, had she lived, she would have been confined to bed or a wheelchair. My mom was a very active woman with six children to raise. She would have suffered so had she lived.

Leslie, three at the time, was the only child with them and received a concussion. Dad received seven broken ribs and other minor injuries. He was allowed out of the hospital to attend the funeral on August 21, 1959.

Only If

    The day of the accident I was babysitting, wondering what all the sirens were about. Dad and Mom would be home soon to watch the *Walt Disney Show* with all of us.

    A neighbor, who was a local police officer in uniform, knocked at the door. I don't remember what he said but that he needed to call a relative. So I gave him Aunt Maryann's number, just about three miles away. Within minutes, our home was full of friends, neighbors, and Aunt Maryann. I was in a daze and don't have any memory of what happened after that.

    I don't know how it happened, but I ended up in the home of my father's sister in Middleton, a short drive away. I remember standing in the kitchen at Aunt Dettie and Uncle Don's. I was being held and kissed and being told about the traffic accident, and that my mother had just died and "it will be alright." I remember being in Aunt Dettie's bed the night of the accident being very, very angry with my mother and asking, "How could you abandon me like this? If only I knew what to do now?" But, I was thirteen and what sensible thoughts can you expect from a child? This was yet another pivotal moment; just another unexpected loss, no time to say goodbye.

    On August 27, I turned fourteen and started high school a few days later. My summer was nothing like what I had in my mind as my last summer as a child. Unfortunately, it was in a twisted way, the end of my childhood. With the death of my mother, I somehow lost my carefree teenage years and made the jump from kid to a young adult with family responsibilities. I was the eldest child, the youngest a baby who was three weeks old. Linda, Leeanna, Lester, Leslie, Louise and Lisa–we were six very sad little children and an infant too young to know the difference just yet.

Only If

Louise, at 18 months, went to live with Aunt June in La Crosse. Lisa, only three weeks, went to live with Aunt Dettie in Middleton. They were two of Dad's sisters. Aunts and uncles on both sides of the family wanted to split us up and help by raising one of the six children. My dad would have no part of adoption or splitting up his family. He only allowed Lisa and Louise to be gone for a few months. He changed his schedule at Oscar Mayer and set up our new living routine, and I was a big part of it from the end of my school day to the time I left the next morning.

Helping Dad take care of our home and family did not mix well with high school responsibilities. By late September, my dad let the principal of Central High School know, in no uncertain terms, that any studying had to be done in school. When I got home, I had household chores to do. Ms. Vida Smith exercised her authority in letting my father know I had an education to acquire.

I spent a lot of time in detention over lunch hours for not having schoolwork completed, so I learned to do my homework in detention or at lunch. It was a show of wills between the principal and my dad, and I was caught in the middle with no control whatsoever. By the time October rolled around, I was ready for an escape.

My escape came from a most unexpected place. Television was still in black and white in those days, and the screen size wasn't much larger than 10 inches by 10 inches, if that. But the lack of color or the size of the screen did not to diminish the exhilarating amazement of *Adventures in Paradise*, starring Gardner McKay.

Each week, the suave and handsome Adam Troy found adventures in the South Seas. His sailing schooner, the Tiki III, traveled to exotic ports of call like Hong Kong, New Guinea, the Fiji Islands, and Pago Pago. The place of my dreams became the white sand beaches of the French Polynesia Islands and the towering palm trees of Tahiti, in particular. Each week my hero would carry people and cargo from one port of call in the South Seas to another.

He would deliver his cargo and save a life or help his passengers solve their problems. He would fight man and nature and evil and emerge each week humble, victorious, and ever so handsome. Yes, his paradise was my paradise and I would live there – someday.

I still get goose bumps when I imagine him at the helm of his schooner, the sails fluttering in the sweetly scented tropical breeze, the azure blue waves breaking at the bow, the winds rippling through his hair, his partially unbuttoned shirt blown flat against his bronze chest and sinuous arms. I suppose he was my very first crush and I was probably experiencing some of the emotions I was told about at the "Mother-Daughter Tea" only a few short months before.

This series lasted from October 1959 to April 1962. However, the effect this singular television show had on me lasted a lifetime. As a teenager, "Adventures in Paradise" was a weekly escape from the grief of my mother's death, an hour away from the realities and responsibilities of a household. It was an hour each week to dream and fantasize and live a life filled with adventure and the possibilities of life.

And then, it would be back to dishes, laundry and ironing (which I hate still today). Later, alone in my bedroom, I would escape each night with three or four cold cut sandwiches. I would have bobby socks on and dance to the radio or my 45 records. I would glide on the linoleum floor and twirl. Or I would lie on my bed and watch the wind blow my sheer curtains. I would imagine the sails billowing in the breeze and dream of a ship and of paradise and Adam, Captain Adam Troy.

By the time fall of 1963 rolled around, I was seventeen, a senior in high school, and extremely overwhelmed. My grades were suffering and my home was chaotic. If only I knew what I was doing, we all would all be so much happier.

I would yell at my brother and sisters and tell them what to do and how to do it "or else." They would just yell back, "You are not my mother. You cannot tell me what to do." And they were so right. Leeanna, the next oldest, was about to turn twelve. Lisa and Louise had long since returned home–Dad wanted all his kids with him. We had clothes on our back, a roof over our heads. We had full stomachs and empty hearts. We were such a sad lot.

My dad was called again to the principal's office at Central High in the fall of 1962. I had been encouraged by school friends to go to the school counselor. I found the strength to talk about my grades and my insecurities with my life at home. She encouraged me to see a social worker.
The social worker encouraged me to confront my father, which was what the meeting was all about. My father stood there listening to the social worker and me. His arms were folded across his chest. The toe of his Oxblood Wingtip shoe was snubbing out an invisible spot on the highly polished floor. He never looked up. My heart broke as he said, "If she does not want to live at home, she doesn't have to." And he left.

I was promised the social worker would act as a mediator so I could speak to my dad. We could develop a plan. But there was no talking with my dad. No opportunity to ask for the help I wanted at home. No negotiations. The decision was made. So be it.

Only If

I was placed in a foster home that day. My mother had abandoned us with her death. My father was in such pain at his loss that he abandoned me. Now I struck another blow for my family and abandoned all of them.

I lived in a foster home for nearly a month. I got to go to my first high school football game with the other girls in the foster home. We used to lie in our bunk beds at night and listen to Dion, Cher, and the Four Seasons. I had responsibilities at the foster home, too, but it was a snap compared to the chores I had at home. At the time, I wondered if anyone even missed me.

After just a few weeks, I moved in with my Aunt Dettie and Uncle Don. Dettie was my father's sister. She had raised Lisa for almost a year. They were a wonderful couple with three older kids of their own. I saw love and respect in their home. I heard calm voices, laughter, and conversations with no raised voices. When one went to the kitchen for a treat, the others were always asked, "Can I bring you something?" This was the life of my dreams. Love, respect, caring, hugs and kisses. It was so good to see how a happy home life was supposed to work.

My aunt and uncle lived about twenty miles from my father and a block away from high school. I transferred to Middleton High as a senior in October of 1962.

Being a transfer student in my senior year, from the state capitol to a small community at that time, did not get me into the cliques at Middleton High School. I spent a lot of time alone. My social skills were not very well developed. I was sort of a loner for the most part, but made friends easily in music class and singing competitions. It was wonderful to go to competitions and other school functions–half a block away or other parts of the state. My grades jumped from C's and D's to A's and B's, and that made me very happy. Maybe I *could* go on to college after all. I so wanted to be a teacher.

Only If

I still enjoyed my music and loved to lie on my bed in the basement and listen to Andy Williams and Johnny Mathis–the two men in the world most responsible for my hormone development at the age of seventeen! I felt safe and loved and felt free to dream of all the possibilities of life, including the South Sea Islands and my Adam Troy.

Hot and humid afternoons during spring vacation in 1963 called for a bike ride to the lake or swimming pool to cool off. Cooler mornings provided just the right temperature for a game of tennis and a long, slow walk to cool off and to catch one's breath after all the physical activity.

One such spring morning, a girlfriend and I were strolling along after a game of tennis, discussing who did what to whom and who is going to where with whom. We meandered along the shady path provided by the bank of towering oak trees, catching the cool and refreshing breeze. Off in the distance two boys disappeared in the ditch, hunting for "pirates" or digging in the "forest" to claim the "buried treasures" as their own.

The boys' game-playing and their banter soon turned to a distressed yell for help. My friend and I picked up our pace to answer the now terrified screams from the ditch. Only one boy was visible. He was standing near the bottom of the hill. His feet, calves and knees had disappeared in the sand. He was babbling incoherently at the top of his lungs. His face was convulsed in fear. His tears etching red streaks on soiled cheeks.

The second boy was nowhere to be found. He was there, somewhere under this heap of sand, earth, twigs and weeds. The three of us began to dig furiously at the heavy, wet soil. The more we dug, the more the clumps fell down from the top of the embankment. More help would be needed if this boy were to be reached in time. I sent the other two for help. They raced off in two different directions, one toward the homes nearby and the other frantically toward the school and tennis courts. I had to have some help somehow.

If only I knew what to do. I just started digging. It seemed like hours but it was only seconds before a shoe, then an ankle, then another leg appeared. Somewhere there should be a waist-here it is! Oh, my God, his eyes are closed! He's not moving! He's not breathing! He's dead!

Loosen his belt. Roll him on his side. Breathe, please breathe! There must be sand in his mouth. Clear it. Put him on his stomach. Turn his head to the side. Arms over his head. Straddle his hips. Put your hands on either side of his waist and glide your hands while pushing up to his armpits over and over again. Come on, breathe!

Did he move? Wait. Wait. Yes, he did! He did! Put him on his side, clear his mouth again. White foam was coming out of his mouth now, but he was coughing, gagging – but breathing! He was breathing!

People were coming from all over now. These men would be able to save him. His eyes were partially opened now. The ambulance could be heard. They would save him.

The three of us were pushed aside while the adults worked on the boy. We all just wandered off without a word said to one another, upset by the recent happenings, not knowing what to say. The young boy disappeared down another street to the far-off scream of the ambulance racing to University Hospital in Madison.

Later that night, in the privacy of my room, I wondered how the boy was. If only I had known what to do. He was only about ten or so. Too young to die. Were the men able to save him? In the middle of my tearful prayers and fears came the voice of my aunt asking me to come to the living room.

There in the center of the living room stood the basketball coach for Middleton High School, Otto Brittenbach. A young boy was at his side. He had come to my aunt's home to thank me for what I had done to save his son's life. The coach's son's life!

Otto Brittenbach went on to coach the University of Wisconsin's Badgers basketball at the Madison campus. A few years later, Coach Brittenbach was able to coach his son, a star basketball player for the Badgers. You see, his son was the real "buried treasure in the sand" that was discovered on that warm spring day in 1963.

This, too, was a pivotal point in my life–but a positive one. This taught me that I can do something right, that I can make a valuable contribution to one man's family. The senior life-saving skills I learned in class could be applied to a sand cave. It did make a difference in someone's life. His life was saved only because I had the courage to take charge and help. I trusted my instincts and did what I thought was right.

I had actually saved a life. This was my first validation as a worthwhile person. This increased my self-worth.

My dream of living on a South Seas island in my own paradise stayed with me all my life. It was my centering point to go to in times of trouble. It was my safe haven. Sometimes I knew I would achieve my dream. Sometimes it seemed a very remote possibility. I had lost my Marcie. I lost my mom. I abandoned my family. But I had saved a life and had a dream to cling to at the tender age of seventeen.

Only If

Becoming a Woman

All the attention I got in school after finding the "buried treasure" was rather nice, I must admit. I finally felt I was a member of the graduating class and part of the community. The seniors were now the leaders, about to go out in the world and make a difference. Time and tide waits for no one, and graduation and destiny were just around the corner.

My mom's family came from Goodman and Madison to my graduation. My aunt had convinced me to invite my dad and he came, too. He handed me a small gift wrapped in tissue paper. I was so nervous my hands were shaking. I did not know what to expect, what to do, what to say. We had not spoken to each other since that day in front of the social worker over seven months ago. As he handed me the gift, I dropped it and it broke. It was a silver wristwatch studded with blue stones on the face. It was never worn and was beyond repair; just like the relationship with my father.

A week or so after graduation, I got an apartment in Madison with my friend, Marsha. We had made it through our senior year together and it only seemed right we room together. We got a two-bedroom duplex on Johnson Street along with the university students.

I was working at the University hospital in a floor kitchen as a food server, assigned to distribute food to patients. The food carts would come to the floor and the patients would come to me and get their trays. Nursing staff would deliver other trays to rooms.

In July 1963, I met the second boy I had ever dated, Larry. We got married the following January, 1964. I was all of eighteen and he was a mere twenty. He had never had his own apartment and had gone from his mother's home to our honeymoon apartment in a small town near Madison.

Marriage was not all I thought it would be. I was hoping for someone who loved me, would care for me, and share my life with. I became the caretaker yet again.

He would pick me up after work and we would drive the twenty miles home. He would often leave again and drive back to Madison to go out drinking and playing pool with his buddies. He returned home late each evening expecting supper to be on the table. We lived on the third floor in a farmhouse. It was the middle of winter and very, very cold.

I remember cuddling in a blanket sitting on the floor for hours, watching the driveway, looking for Larry's car to come down farm road. As soon as it did, I jumped to my feet and took our dinner from the oven where it had been since 6 p.m. No microwave oven in those days – just a low gas stove. Being the people-pleasing person I am, the food was hot, arranged at a table, catering to his every need. We ate late, but at least we were together.

We moved several times those first few years. Larry kept changing jobs and we could not make the rent, constantly needing to find another home. In 1965, we packed our belongings and moved to California and lived in El Monte. A buddy heard of work in the aerospace field, so we moved.

It was nice to be in a climate with no snow, lemon and fig trees, and halfway between the coast and the arid desert. We were doing much better. Steady work and steady pay. After about six months, we drove straight back to Madison. Larry's mom said she was very ill and we drove for two days without stopping. As we came into her home, she pointed out that Larry left behind a pack of cigarettes. She was not terminal; just plain sick.

Through the first six years of our marriage, I spent many evenings alone. I had time to read, listen to music, and found comfort again eating my cold cut sandwiches and dreaming of living on a tropical island. The dream seemed to be an immature childhood whim – only a memory and just a remote possibility. But still, it would be nice "if only."

Our daughter, Michelle, came along in March 1971. We were talking about the possibility of adoption, but had little confidence we would qualify with Larry's work record and me doing waitress jobs and some grill-work.

And then, there she was; brown hair, blue eyes, and with the plumpest of cheeks. She reminded me of photos I had seen of my mother as a young girl. We gave Michelle the nickname of "chipmunk cheeks."

It was so wonderful to have this beautiful little thing in my arms. I was fearful that I would not make a good mother – I had proven that already with my brother and sisters. But my little "chipmunk cheeks" filled me with feelings of accomplishment, joy and contentment, and the love and blissful acceptance I had always yearned for.

In December 1971, we were renting a home on a lake in McFarland, Wisconsin, not far from Madison. Michelle began to walk all by herself. I coaxed Larry to take Michelle by the hand and walk her to her first Christmas tree. The tree was fresh cut by us and turned out lovely. Our favorite decorations we had chosen over the years adorned the boughs. It was our first child's first Christmas.

I sat there watching the two of them touching the icicles and blowing at them to watch them shimmer in the pretty twinkling multi-colored lights.

Then Larry noticed something especially for him. I had cut letters out and strung them on a string of yarn and placed it as a banner around the tree: "Merry Christmas New Dad To Be."

After waiting for seven years for Michelle, we were blessed with our Larry Michael Jr. in July 1972. Two kids just fifteen months apart.

Michael's birth was very quick and event-free. Heck, I hardly made it to the hospital in time for either of them with a combined total of seven hours of labor! But there was a problem within a few hours of his birth.

The first time I was able to have him in my room, I examined him from head to toe – as all new moms and dads do. I noticed he seemed to have problems breathing and rang for the nurse. Apparently, Michael's lungs had not expelled all the mucus from birthing and he contracted pneumonia. This robust seven-and-a-half pound boy was twice the size of most of the premature babies in St Mary's Hospital.

It was very difficult standing outside the shaded windows of the neonatal unit and telling my family what to expect when we went inside. There he was, hooked up to monitors with tubes and wires patched all over his little body.

I had to go home after three days and Michael was in the hospital for seven more. I did not drive and we lived in McFarland, too far away for Larry to drive home and take me into Madison. Larry visited Michael daily after work.

The call finally came and we were told we could take our son home. I called the babysitter and we were on our way. I had been thinking and planning for this day. We stopped and bought Michelle a baby doll to give her when she was introduced to her brother.

Only If

The plan worked well. Every time I changed Larry's diaper, Michelle changed her baby. We fed them together and when my baby went to bed, she placed her baby in her buggy. I remember one day when I was changing the diaper and Larry Sr. was calling out Larry Jr.'s name, Michelle looked at Daddy, looked at the baby and looked at Daddy again. Suddenly she blurted out, "He is Larry (pointing to Daddy) and he is Michael." And so be it.

We now had Larry and Michael and Michelle and Linda in our home. Those two years I was able to stay at home with my children were wonderful. I could be a mom and love and enjoy my kids. And I did. At last I had a home on the lake and was loved and accepted by my kids.

But time passes and no matter how many kids a family has, no child can ever cover up the problems in a marriage. My husband had a drinking problem since the day I meant him. I always thought I could help him through his personal problems and make him happy. If only I knew how.

He had a hard time holding down a job for very long. I could only call in for him and make excuses a few times before he was fired for missing days yet again. Thank goodness we had insurance when Michael was born. Insurance paid the entire cost of Michael's birth and prolonged hospital stay: $1,295.

But there were many other bills that needed to be paid. The kids were sick all the time, lung problems for Michael and colds for Michelle. Larry was in and out of the hospital for various problems, all without a job or insurance. I had to go back to work and help support my family, pay off the pile of bills, and try to salvage our marriage as well.

My dreams of college never happened due to my mother's death. All that was easily available for an overweight high school graduate with two kids were waitressing or cook positions. I was at the bottom of the ladder with nowhere to go but up.

I made pretty good money in tips and by putting in a full day, but we barely got by. If only I had a better education, I would be able to provide for my family. If only he did not drink, he could hold down a job. If only I were a slimmer, better person, he said he would not drink anymore.

Through the years of repeated unemployment, we somehow managed to come up with a plan that worked for us for a time. When we both had a job, daycare costs took one of our wages. So we decided Larry would stay home and take care of the kids. I became the breadwinner. He was a good father and loved his children–no one could deny. By expanding my workday to ten or twelve hours, we were actually able to start to pay off some bills. I took extra hours at the restaurant, making omelets for breakfast and turning into a hostess at lunchtime on Saturday and Sunday.

We had a roof over our heads, clothes on our backs, and we took the kids to the doctor when needed. But I was so tired.

Over the next few years, I no longer had any respect for my husband – or myself, for that matter. Gone was the dream of a white picket fence around our home in the country. There would never be a knight in shining armor to rescue me. Gone was the dream of my tropical island. Gone was any hope.

Was this all there really was to life? What can I do to make it better? I had no clue. I was lost, alone and depressed with no one to talk to.

~

One day in early spring 1977, while driving home from work, I decided this would be the day. This would be the day I would end my life. My husband and kids would be much better off without me.

Only If

I had thought of all the ways one could end one's life. Pills? No, I took no prescriptions except for birth control. Never heard of anybody overdosing on birth control and I worked far too hard to use illegal drugs. I had read of people slitting their wrists and considered it for a time, but passed on that too. I had thought of a gun, but all we had were Larry's hunting rifles. Try as I did (with an empty gun) I could not figure out how to manage it. My arms were too short to place it under my chin and pull the trigger. This seemed to be a little messy and I did not want anyone to have to do the cleanup. Then it came to me, a car accident.

I had lost many loved ones in car accidents. They all died. I would, too. As I traveled back and forth on the West Beltline Highway each day, I watched for the perfect place, a place to end it all and yet have the least possibility of killing anyone else, with a high probability of taking my life and ending this unhappiness and depression.

It would be the John Nolen Drive exit. The guardrails were cement, but low. I figured if I got the car up to 80 or 85 miles per hour, I would break through the rail, sail over the boulevard underneath, and hit the concrete walls.

I was within one mile of the designated interchange. One and a half miles from the home we had before my mom died in 1959. And just three miles from my home and two kids.

Then I remembered. I just got paid today. I would go home and get the check there for my family and I would do this all tomorrow.

I became very peaceful and calm. My kids would get the paycheck and my husband could find a better woman, and all this pain and suffering would end tomorrow.

Only If

Something came over me traveling those three miles to my home. Guess it was one of those moments when there is only one set of footprints in the sand, and God was taking care of me in my deepest moment of despair.

I don't know how I got home, but I remember parking the car. I remember putting my purse and check on the table. I walked to the kitchen, opened the drawer and got the phone book. I looked up the number of my OBGYN and asked for an appointment today. It was near closing time and the nurse would not set up an appointment for today.

I told her I almost killed myself three miles ago. I need to see a doctor NOW. I was in his office fifteen minutes later.

For some crazy reason, the nurse gave me a paper garment and asked me to take off my clothes and sit on the exam table. I complied, powerless to object.

The doctor came and while washing his hands told me to lie down. He then put my feet in the stirrups and started to give me a vaginal exam. I asked what he was doing and he said he was doing a pelvic exam and a pap smear. I asked what a pap smear had to so with me wanting to kill myself.

He stopped immediately. Finally he asked why I came today. I told him I was going to kill myself forty-five minutes ago. I called for help, not a pap smear.

He removed his gloves, washed and told me to get dressed and he would be back in a few minutes.

He was very kind. I cried and he listened. It was well after dark when our conversation ended. My doctor made me sign a contract that night. A contract to promise I would not kill myself tonight and a promise to keep the appointment he made with a shrink for me for 9 o'clock the next morning.

Fortunately, it was my day off, and when I make a commitment to someone, I keep it.

So the days of visiting a doctor after work, three for four times a week, began. Drug therapy started and the pain was finally gone. I got up and went to work. Ten or twelve hours later I came home, sat in the chair with my two kids on my lap, and fell asleep holding them. Then I went to bed. I was like a machine each day, never missing a doctor's appointment. He knew I had no money to pay him, but asked me to continue to come.

I learned a lot those few months. Learned things about my life and the death of my mother I had yet to deal with. Learned about my relationship with my father and siblings, and got clues how to either cure it or let it go. I learned about my husband's mental and medical problems. I discovered his medical problems were caused by his lifestyle and not "who I was" as a human being, which is what I had been told for twelve years. It had more to do with being a smoker and drinker starting back when he was ten or twelve years old. I learned that I was not lazy or dumb or stupid or too fat. I learned all the tapes that played nightly in my mind were all the hurts and unresolved issues my soul wanted to deal with.

My mind had to face it, too, if I was going to have any happiness at all or find a desire to live.

One day at work at Country Kitchen in Madison, I was carrying forty-eight hardboiled eggs that I had just cooled off in the restaurant sink. I was walking over to my workstation and slipped on the tile floor.

There I was, in all my glory, sitting spread eagle on the prep room floor. Forty-eight little eggs rocking, rolling and waddling in a concentric circle toward the drain in the floor. It was the funniest thing I had ever seen in my entire life!

Only If

I was laughing at the little roly-poly eggs as the restaurant manager helped me onto my feet. He walked me back to the break area and asked if I was all right.

I stopped laughing and said, "This is the first time in months and months I have been alright. Can I leave for the day?"

Moments later, I was in the car heading for the shrink's office. I waited a few minutes until his current appointment finished. Once in the office, I threw the bottle of pills at his chest and said, "I do not want nor do I need these anymore." He said he was waiting for me to tell him that.

I sat down and we talked. I told him I would rather live in pain than be numb. I had embarrassed myself at work with the egg incident. I wanted to take control of my emotions again. He told me about withdrawing from the prescription. If I followed his plan, I would be off the pills completely in a month.

I went home that day and told my husband I wanted a divorce. He knew I was serious and it took only a couple weeks for him to find a job after being unemployed all these years. Larry got his own apartment and moved out for a June rental, taking our car with him.

A few weeks later, on June 19, 1977, my only brother, Mark (Lester Mark) died at the age of twenty-two in yet another car accident – the bane of our family.

I was very glad I still had some of those pills in my system to lean on one last time. The agony of seeing my father's pain at the loss of his only son was equal to the pain I was carrying at the loss of my mother. It was not a pretty sight, but easy to recognize and feel.

This was one of those pivotal moments yet again. Death of a marriage; death of a brother. I chose to withdraw and hide. I withdrew to the small town of Oconto in Northeastern Wisconsin, many miles and hours away from Madison and all the bad memories. After living in Oconto for a few months, I found a three-bedroom home to rent on the bay of Green Bay right next to the water.

The water was so peaceful. It was a constant in my life. The morning sunrise filled my life with hope with each new day that was given to me. There was a Ben Franklin stove to snuggle up to on the sofa with my two children. All I wanted to do was snuggle with my kids, be sure the clouds rolled by in the right direction, and the waves lapped repeatedly against the shoreline as my two rug rats and I watched the birds and little animals and all the glories of God's creation.

We had such a good life there. Michele and Michael loved to fish with a piece of corn or worm on the hook. We had a long driveway to the road, and Michael learned to ride his bike there.

There were miles of sandy beaches to walk, thunderstorms to watch forming and move across the bay, raining as they traveled. A couple times we even saw "water spouts" form off Sturgeon Bay to the east. A water spout is a water-based little tornado. There was so much of God's nature to enjoy.

I was receiving Aid to Families with Dependent Children (AFDC) to supplement the small wage I earned working in a kitchen for $2.50. I was a cook and averaged 225 pounds of perch for a Friday night fish fry and a full menu. We did not have much, but we were happy.

I came to wonder if dealing with emotional pain and loss is like living with rheumatoid arthritis. The arthritis eats away at the soft joint tissues of the body. The disease can be treated with medications, but the arthritis will still run its course until it burns itself out. The pain may eventually go away with arthritis, but your joints are left damaged and disfigured. Only major surgery can replace the devastated joints.

And so it is with emotional pain and loss. It can be tempered with medications, counseling and treatments. But ultimately, the pain and loss needs to be dealt with, too. It needs to be faced and felt, or our heart and soul can become damaged and disfigured. Pain and loss want to be recognized, honored and validated, and then we can bless and release the pain and memories. Only then can we forgive. Only then can we begin to heal and renew our soul.

All this pain and suffering was not the life I wanted for my two small children or for me. I did not want to pass on the burden I carried of low self-esteem, negative thought patterns and not feeling worthy to those I love. Something had to change.

My first change was to moving to Oconto and starting the healing process. The second was getting an education.

I had been smart enough to go back to vocational school in 1979 and earn a bookkeeping degree. I worked hard to increase my bookkeeping skills. I used to do some bookkeeping for my employer, but I needed to make myself more marketable to earn more money.

Guess I was not "stupid" after all. This 35-year-old lady managed a 3.87 grade-point average and was voted the Outstanding Student of the Year in 1979 at Northeast Wisconsin Technical College (NWTC). I went to school making $2.50 per hour cash at the Club Oconto. My first job after graduation from NWTC was $6.25 per hour. Who said education does not pay? I am prof that it does pay, "Only If" you work for that prize.

Only If

Changing My Thoughts, Changing My Life

My dream of a tropical paradise stayed alive somehow.

I remember one year Michelle did research on Tahiti for a school project. She researched the people, land mass, location, flag, climate and gross national product. She drew maps and cut pictures out of magazines. It was so nice to share this dream of paradise with my daughter; to laugh and giggle at what we might experience if only we went there.

I went to NWTC in 1979 and 1980 to get my account clerk degree. A bookkeeper's job is to follow state and federal mandates for recording the revenue (income) and expenses (how you spend income) for clients and customers. You reconcile bank statements, lease agreements, purchase orders and invoices for their customer services, and create monthly statements summarizing the information. The accountant uses this information for tax preparation and helping business owners make financial decisions.

I did banking and inventory for most of my employers and wanted to see if I could become an educated bookkeeper. And so I did.

I drove to school five days a week for nine months. I went to school under the "Win/Win" program President Reagan's administration designed for someone just like me, underemployed and needing a hand-up, not a hand-out.

I received a stipend for living expenses, money for travel expenses, allotment for school supplies, including an adding machine. I never could have afforded these expenses on $2.50 per hour as a cook, waitress or bartender.

At long last, I got an education. It happened with a childhood dream and "Only If" I asked for and accepted help from my case worker.

I found confidence and self-esteem. I discovered I was not stupid, as I had been called in grade school and high schools by my husband and my father. I had been given responsibilities I had not been trained to do. I could pour a bowl of cereal or heat up a can of soup and make cold cut sandwiches. Julia Child's PBS show helped me learn about cooking.

If you don't know what you are doing, one can appear to be stupid rather than unfamiliar and untrained. I got seventeen out of eighteen A's in vocational school at the age of thirty-five. I was not stupid. When I am taught, I do learn and use that information to improve life for my clients, myself and my kids.

My case worker helped me find a job in Green Bay, Wisconsin, after I graduated. To save on expenses, Michelle, Michael and I moved from our healing home on the bay to a duplex off Lombardi Avenue with the Green Bay Packers' famous stadium, Lambeau Field, in plain view.

I was working five days a week. The kids were going to Beaumont Elementary School a few blocks from our home, and our little family unit worked in the yard together on Saturdays. I motivated my kids with a reward of a hot shower and going across the street for Pizza Hut and sodas. Michelle took clarinet lessons and babysat. Michael played baseball for a Schneider National team, and we got a cat named Isaac. Life was good for us.

I started teaching my kids how to make some family food favorites. They loved that. I would make extra meals on the weekend and freeze them. I taught both kids how to set the oven on 250 degrees and heat our dinner that I took out in the morning. I would call them and let them know how to turn on the oven and put the meal in, and when to turn it up to 350 degrees to make it hot for dinner when I got home.

When I arrived from work, they were usually doing their homework with a little help if needed after dinner was done. I would set the table and make a salad and hot vegetable, and we were ready to eat in thirty minutes.

In 1980, my long-standing back problem became more severe. I used to carry two or three cases of beer bottles at a time and had been overworking my back for years. It finally got so bad the doctor wanted to fuse my fourth and fifth lumbar discs together. The disc was shattered and it seemed the only answer to the recurring pain.

My current employer suggested against back surgery. She had had an unsuccessful experience, but I could no longer stand the pain. Due to the ninety-day recovery expected, I lost my job.

Time off from work was a blessing in disguised. My ex-husband was trying to get his child support of $100 per month cut in half. Since I was trained to be a bookkeeper, I kept excellent records and all receipts. I created a spreadsheet of all the expenses that came in support of our children and was able to document that I provided 83 percent of their food, housing, clothing, school, music, sports needs and entertainment. His request for support decrease was not approved.

Only If

After sixty days of recovery, I could hardly stand the inactivity and started searching for full-time employment. I found a new job three blocks from our home as a bookkeeper for JF Hennig Associates. They bought and sold gold and silver for investments, purchased estate jewelry, and Jim Hennig was a successful motivational speaker.

I worked for this family business from 1980 to 1985. It was at his office when I worked off the clock to learn databases and spreadsheets to "improve my marketability" to earn more money. Of course, I increased what I was able to do for him as we developed a database for his motivational speaking business, too.

To earn more money, I started doing bookkeeping after work for a few clients. Jim sent a client my way. I found two other part-time clients, and once the kids went to bed, I turned the kitchen table into my "office" and worked until 11 o'clock or midnight and on weekends.

Life got better and better for my family. I kept track of my new income, created a budget and put money in the bank for upcoming expenses.

In addition to upcoming expenses, I would put $20 to $50 aside monthly for fun with my kids. Some money went for trips to Green Bay's Bay Beach Amusement Park, the movies, county fairs, Great America, and even to a cabin on a lake with a fishing boat about an hour from Green Bay.

We drove to Goodman to visit my grandma and Rhinelander to visit my girlfriend, Sheila, and her family. Our family loved to go to the duck pond with bags of bread. We ended this adventure with our own picnic lunch on a blanket. When we fed the ducks in the winter, we had our lunch in the back seat of the car. We also saved money by shopping at Goodwill and St. Vincent de Paul. The kids recycled cans. We worked well together toward common goals. Life was good.

Only If

There was never much visiting between me and my four sisters who lived around Madison. My father came to my home once in 1971 for Michelle's baptism. That was it.

So in 1984, I accepted an invitation from my sister, Louise, to spend Easter weekend with all the trimmings at her home in southern Wisconsin. My father, sisters, and nieces and nephews would be there, too.

Louise had a batch of three-month-old lab mix puppies. The kids chased them all around the country property. Louise loves to take photos, the kids chased the dogs and everyone had a good time. We decided to have Easter dinner on Saturday since everyone was famished and ready to relax. Saturday was our day to celebrate, so Easter Sunday was spent with my sister's in-laws.

A composite photo of Michael, me and Michelle

The kids were all between eight and twelve years old. We laughed and got reconnected. Everyone went home later while Michelle, Michael and I stayed overnight. Sometime after they were asleep, Louise and I realized, "What about the Easter Bunny?" I never gave it a thought – no supplies were purchased, no baskets, no goodies! For me, the visit was all about reconnecting with my family.

Only If

Louise came to the rescue and had extra green grass. I folded down a couple shopping bags and we made nests for the goodies. She saved the day for the Easter Bunny and my kids. We hid the baskets and put out the colored eggs, and she even hid a few eggs for the kids to find. I awoke to the smell of fresh coffee and excited kids wondering if the Easter Bunny would find us since we were not in our home in Green Bay. But we did get a visit!

In the pre-dawn hours it began to snow. Snow! On April 22nd! Spring in Wisconsin can bring all sorts of weather, and now we got five inches of snow. Saturday was clear and more like fall, with brown grass and autumn leaves moving in the wind. Easter Sunday had snow that covered the Easter Bunny tracks and displayed new deer tracks in the fresh snow.

Louise and I spent most of the morning eating breakfast and sharing pots of coffee. The kids enjoyed the Easter goodies and munched on hard-boiled eggs. We all got dressed and prepared to make the four-hour drive back to Green Bay. It had stopped snowing for about three hours. The sky was blue and the landscape was beautiful, a sight to linger over and enjoy.

We loaded the car, accepted a little lunch Louise packed for us, said our goodbyes and filled up on hugs and kisses. It had been the first Easter Sunday with my family for nearly twenty years. It all went so well.

We drove about an hour and a half to Madison and stopped at a gas station for the kids to wish Happy Easter to their Grandmother Dorothy. We could not call their dad because he and his wife were traveling in far western Wisconsin. Michael hit the restroom, the kids changed seats and buckled up. Michael went to the back seat and Michelle moved to the front – we always had to have seat assignments to keep peace on trips.

Only If

I was tailing a snowstorm that had gone through only three hours before. The roads were snow-free and nearly dry – the snowplows did a good job as the snow moved from south to north.

I turned off Highway 151 in favor of Highway 26 through the small town of Rosendale. The well-traveled Highway 26 is a popular short cut between Madison, the Fox Cities and Green Bay. It was plowed and salted, busy with travelers making their way to Easter festivities, but not dry like the four-lane divided Highway 151.

I passed through Rosendale traveling north. Michael was snoozing in the back seat and Michelle was leaning against the door, snuggled into her pillow. It was such a beautiful and scenic road with snow-covered pine trees, fences with snow on top of rails and posts, flocks of birds flying here and there, and good music on the radio.

My car found some black ice as we came over a rolling hill at the top of a crest. I remember seeing the pale green roofs of a farm to my right, and then nothing.

When I awoke, there were no windows left in the car. Michael and I were in the back seat. I got out of the back seat and into the driver's seat, and saw Michelle sitting up straight with her head tilted to the side. Her eyes were fluttering and I heard a little gurgle sound, and then nothing.

Michelle died almost instantly. It was Michelle's turn in the front seat. She must have unfastened her seat belt after we left Madison to call Grandma Hamm. She had snuggled into her pillow to sleep. I never did look at the death certificate. It mattered not how she died, only that she had died. If someone has to die, Easter Sunday of 1984 was a perfect day to ascend into heaven.

Only If

Michael, stilled buckled in, sprained his foot and ankle and was on crutches for a time. I got a cut on my left hand, picked lots of shattered glass from my permed hair, and had my heart broken. I lived for many years with the guilt of causing the death of my Michelle.

Witnesses said that as my car came over the crest of the hill, I was spinning in slow motion across the lanes of traffic. A cargo van ended up perpendicular to the road with his back end facing north in the ditch. My car hit the cargo van's front end with the passenger door. That was that.

Many travelers provided emergency assistance. EMTs, doctors and nurses stopped to provide assistance, but none was needed. Pats on my shoulder, kind words and prayers were given. Someone put me in the back seat with Michael again and covered us with a blanket we had. I remember policemen and hearing an ambulance siren, and holding Michael's hand and saying a prayer. We were moved to another car and I remember seeing a woman opening the car door to tend to Michelle. She removed her stethoscope and shook her head. Michelle was gone.

Everything else is a blur. I remember an officer asked if I had been drinking. It was 1:30 on a Sunday! I said I had a glass of wine with dinner yesterday and pots of coffee this morning.

Michelle left in an ambulance. An officer took us to the hospital. Someone asked for my driver's license and insurance card, and wanted me to sign permission for an autopsy. I approved them to do what was required by law, but I said, "Don't cut her up and don't tell me about it." I asked if we could donate her organs, but they said it was too late. God, what a mess.

Michael cried for loss of his Easter basket. The staff at the hospital put a collection of goodies they had for Easter and gave Michael his new basket, and not a folded-down paper bag one. They were so kind.

Only If

I asked about the other driver and they took me to his room after they got his permission. I had to apologize to him for the accident. He, too, was kind and forgiving. I did not deserve all this kindness.

I remember being asked if I wanted to see Michelle, but replied no. I did not deserve to see her and say my goodbyes. I felt I was not worthy.

I remember being led to a phone and looking in my purse for my sister's phone number in Madison. We needed a ride, since my car was totaled. I remember calling my sister, Leeanna, for a ride and told her I totaled my car and Michelle did not make it.

She asked, "What do you mean she did not make it?"

"She is gone," I said.

I handed the phone to the officer and they made arrangements to take Michael and me to the Juneau County line, where Leeanna could take us to her home and my family waiting for us in Madison. They stopped at McDonald's for a burger and fries for Michael. It had been many hours since lunch and it was now dark out.

Where did it all go? Reconnecting with my family on Holy Saturday and the disconnection of my own little family on Easter Sunday.

Life no longer was good.

I remember my father taking me in his arms and saying, "You did not deserve this." I now understood what his pain was with the death of his wife and his only son, Mark, in 1977. Someone asked if I had told Larry yet. I responded I did not know where he was in Wisconsin. Leeanna knew someone who worked with his wife. The coworker got hold of her and they called them. Soon enough, Larry called me, and I had to tell him what I did. We waited so many years for our children and now one was gone.

Only If

I remember waking up in my sister's waterbed. I was warm, comfortable and peaceful, and then I woke up and it all came back to me in flashes. Michelle with her arms full of puppies, the fall day, the snow, the windowless car the sounds of the sirens and the faces of strangers full of grace, the hospital staff, my family, the first glimpse of Michelle moments after the accident. Please let me forget. Please God, please! All my family was with me to share our sorrow.

I remember sitting on the padded edge of her waterbed wondering, "What do I do now? Why was I saved and Michelle taken from us? What else does God have in mind for me, for us?" The only thing I could do that first day was go to a mall and find some eye makeup to cover my two black eyes.

Most of the memories the next few days are brief moments of pain and guilt. Larry and his wife picked Michael and I up and took us to their home on night two. Renee watched Michael while Larry and I chose the casket and arranged for her services in his church in Madison. That is where our families were for the most part. My family in Goodman drove the four hours south for the services.

I remember the closing of the casket at the funeral home. I remember pacing across the back of the room and down the sides. One by one, people left their seats and gathered outside the room, giving me space to grieve.

I finally worked up the courage to walk up to the casket and say goodbye and ask for her forgiveness yet again. I then took my place next to Larry and Michael.

Then, as if on cue, the funeral director came into the room with the people that had collected in the outer room. He invited people to pay their final respects before closing the casket. I had to go to the casket yet again.

Only If

The priest did his part and that was that. We all went to the gravesite. When service was completed, the casket lowered to the flowers at ground level, we were invited to leave. Thank God I did not have to see her covered with soil. I think I rode with Larry to the reception. I remember I now felt at peace.

My brother-in-law, Steve Hamm, and his wife, Monica, drove Michael and I back to Green Bay. It was very kind of them to deliver us home.

We chatted all the way back to Green Bay. Once their car was unloaded, no one could find a word to express our sorrow and love. We exchanged hugs and kisses, and said our goodbyes. The day after we got home, I got a phone call for Michelle. I was dumbfounded, what to say. But I gave a brief comment about her accident. Sometime that week, a Girl Scout came over to my home with a crafted wreath wall decoration in shades of pale orange and pink.

Rising kids, dating and marriage do not come with a road map or plan of action. Neither does burying a child. Whatever you do to get through these experiences is the right thing to do. Whatever you need to do to cope is alright. It is your right, your privilege, your way.

The next two years I got lost in my job. In 1986, a friend of mine, Doris, got this deal through AARP for a companion fare. For only $100, I could go with her to Hawaii as a companion! I somehow managed to get her to combine her fare of $600 and my $100 fare and divide it by two, and she allowed me to pay $350 instead of $100.

Now, in retrospect, I was so dumb. Six hundred dollars for airfare and hotel accommodations? But, I was in a lost world filled with guilt and grief in those days. This sensitive and compassionate lady knew I did not have much money at $6.25 per hour and she concocted this story to take me on a vacation to Hawaii. She knew my dream of living on a tropical island and found an island that was affordable to her via AARP. What a friend she was to me. What a gift she gave me. She gave me my dream again.

She never knew the life-altering ramifications that vacation in paradise had on me, for she died a few years later. Once I spent that week on Maui, I just knew this was the island of my dreams. Instead of the South Seas, I moved my dream 20 degrees north of the equator to Maui, Hawaii. It was everything I ever imagined my paradise to be and so much more. This was the place where I would live eventually.

This was the place I found my center again and rediscovered God. We had taken the tour to Hana on a nine-passenger tour bus. We drove right to the ocean's edge in those days and to the mouth of the ancient lava flow. I picked my way down to a rock in the middle of the gully.

I sat there facing the vastness of the Pacific Ocean spread out before me. The pale aqua-green waves slammed against my boulder and the walls of the valley created by the lava flow. Sprays of salt water cooled my body. Sea foam created by the force of the turbulent waves attached to my shoes, pants and hair.

Suddenly, I could see myself sitting on this rock! (a Shirley MacLaine-style, out-of-body experience.) The surf was pounding the rocks and shoreline. I looked up from the lava flow and saw twenty-one pools, and not the seven I heard were there. I saw the majesty of Haleakala towering at 10,023 feet. I was crying out to God with all the pain and sorrow I held deep within me for two years, "God, oh God, why did you take her away from me? What did I ever do to deserve this punishment?"

Then suddenly I heard His voice. He told me, "You will heal, but it will take time. You will heal, but it will take time."

Only If

I had this overwhelming feeling of peace, love and contentment come over me. It is a gift I took with me from Maui, and it has been a centering point or goal over all these years. I knew I achieved it once He placed it in my soul to let me know those feelings. Those feelings became my centering point. On this magical island of Maui at the Sacred Pools of O'hiao, I found unconditional love. I wanted to become the person who received unconditional love, but more importantly, one who gave unconditional love.

Hawaii may have become my personal paradise in 1986, but my $6.25 wage was not going to get me too far. It was barely enough to get me in and around Green Bay, Wisconsin, and support my fourteen-year-old son and me.

I was doing bookkeeping at home at night after Michael went to bed. This was a great supplement to our lifestyle in those days. But if I wanted to move to paradise, I would need to make more money. To command more money, I needed to improve my skills.

I had been doing bookkeeping on the side to earn some money to help to support us. I put in unpaid time at the office to learn more about the word processing package and spreadsheet program my employer had on his system. The better my skills, the more money I could command.

Steve, my tax accountant, knew of my dreams and directed me toward a goal-setting package he used. He received this package at a training seminar a few years before and it had served him well. He gave me a copy and assured me it would help me reach my goals. I took the package, but was not very impressed. All these lifestyle and personal choice questions, goals for work, goals for home, relationship goals – toss that one out for sure. At forty-one, I had heard it all: "In order to achieve a goal, you first need to set one." And then there is "Anything the mind can conceive, you can achieve." Yada, yada, yada.

I had heard all this stuff long ago, but I knew it was not about setting goals for me. Everything in life costs money. I knew it was all about making money. I needed money to make it to Hawaii, not to set a goal!

Well, as usual, was I ever wrong. I needed to change my attitude if I wanted to change my life! I slowly came to the realization that the more money I made, the more money I spent.

I said "uncle" and threw in the towel, and opened the goal-setting package again. I started out slowly and set modest increases in my annual income, and the first year it was more than I had planned. So I increased it even more, and lo and behold at the end of year two, it was more than I had dreamed possible.

I adopted October as my time to set goals. I do so love fall in northern Wisconsin. It is my favorite season. The earth is filled with warm colors of the changing hardwoods. The air is fresh and pure again with the freezing temperatures at night, and the earth is washed clean by the autumn rains. Sometimes I could smell the wood-burning fireplaces in the neighborhood and would be whisked back to pleasant memories of my early childhood in Goodman.

So, one weekend in October, I piled all the pillows I owned on the bed. I even made a ceramic coffee carafe with a candle burner that sat on the nightstand for my "goal setting weekend." The east and south-facing bedroom windows would be opened as far as the weather permitted for comfort. Goal-setting time was here.

Each year I would answer the same questions from the year before. I would use clean paper to record my answers. When I was all done with this year's plans, I would look at last year and see how far I had come. I would look at prior years to see what I had achieved. I would write down the month I had accomplished the goal.

Spurred on by my successes, I would then take another look at my goals for the next year, and motivated by the prior year's successes, I would upgrade the next year's goals. Always increasing the income I wanted and demanding more in my personal and spiritual expectations.

It always amazed me how things got done. In my personal goals, I just wrote them down and never looked at them again until the next October. Every time I tried to break down the tasks into monthly goals, I would become demotivated when I did not get them done in the time frame I had set. So I just stop setting monthly goals. Just setting annual goals worked best for me. Somehow they always came true. And it came true because I put it in my mind. Making choices are easy if it takes you toward your goal. First, you have to have the goal!

In my business life, it was easy to set monthly or quarterly goals because in 1987, I became a business owner and I was more in control of the outcome. I would set goals for equipment purchases and the money would magically appear. I would create a desire for a new client and the new client would call. Of course, I had to write a letter and follow up and advertise, but once I created the desire for more business, that desire was filled. Amazing!

In 1987, I also built a home. I was a single parent and the owner of a small business with seven employees, me, the bookkeeper. I owned a business and built a new home. Wow! That was a childhood dream, too, and now it came true.

Only If

In 1990, I joined a support group at Nativity Parish in Green Bay. I did so in support of a friend of mine. Little did I know I was the one who needed this class the most.

It is strange and somewhat uncomfortable to be with a group of people who practice unconditional love. I did not know what that skill was, but had felt it on Maui. This was my opportunity to cultivate and master this skill.

As is the custom in such groups, all things are confidential. People were comfortable sharing. By sharing with one another, we can learn that our feelings and wants are worthy and real. We can learn our lessons in life through the pain of others or not. It is our choice.

In April of 1991, as part of the support group activity, I wrote a letter to my daughter. It was called "Seven Years." Now that I look back at it, I find it was drafted on April 22, the anniversary of her death. At last I was able to verbalize what I had done to my daughter. At last I was able to express my pent-up feelings. It was the largest step forward I had ever taken. Here is that letter:

Seven Years Later

It has been seven years now since you've gone. Sometimes I wonder where all the years have gone. Slowly but surely, second by second, they have all slipped through my fingertips.

I was looking back over some old Day Timers a few weeks ago and discovered it's been seven years. I thought it had only been four. It's hard to put a finger on where the other three years had gone.

Numbness is the only word that comes to mind. About two years after you left, I remember looking through the files at the office and I had no recollection of a great deal of the information they contained.

Something in my subconscious must have taken over and done all this work for me. To my great surprise, it was done very well. Letters were constructed well. Follow-up steps were taken. Everything seemed to be in order, just the way the job was supposed to be done.

Remember how I always mindlessly doodled when I was troubled or confused? You should have seen some of the call back reports! My standard scenes of trees, hills and meandering streams were all over the margins. Bet my boss must have thought me a real nut case with all those pictures in the margins of his client's files.

Doesn't matter what he thought. Sometimes the silliest things help me to survive a crisis. The flowing water and things in nature are always soothing to me. Don't know what I would have done without the reassurance and consistency of nature. The world spins on its axis, waves gently roll to the shore, the clouds move west to east. Time and tides wait for no one.

All through my life I walked around with "guilt" plastered on my forehead. Whenever anything went wrong, I always managed to take responsibility for the action in some way. Even if I was not directly involved in the occurrence, somehow I must have been part of the cause.

This reflex action was very much a part of my life. I often wondered how I developed this deep sense of guilt. It must have come from somewhere in my childhood. I do know I often thought I was not loved. I was often criticized for the tasks I did. No remembered compliments, only complaints.

A child really needs to have some positive reinforcement and guidance to know they are "correctly" performing. Somehow there must be an avenue for self-confidence to develop. The avenue needs to come from a parent or a family network. A little child does not have confidence as an instinct. It is a learned trait.

It's difficult to be far past thirty-nine and constantly questioning your every action, wondering if you are performing correctly, properly, or in an acceptable manner. Confidence is the belief in you, the ability to trust your judgments, the conviction of your principles without worry of recourse. To have your opinions listened to and respected if not for their content, at least for your right to form an opinion and your right to express it.

Guilt lived long in my life; the very bane of my existence. It colored each decision I made. Was I worthy? Did I deserve anything because of what I had done? I was guilt personified.

Guilt is no longer my consistent companion. This is strange feeling. Is it all right to let go of the burden of guilt? How long does one "do" penance? Are seven years of torment, anguish, grief, regret, remorse, and endless hours of bone-weary emptiness enough? Are sleepless nights filled with nightmares and daydreams filled with flashbacks enough? How do you know it is time to end the guilt?

It is time to end when I realize and accept I am human, and as a human I can, do, and will make mistakes. Some mistakes are minor ones, some mistakes have far-reaching results. If I make a mistake, the action is an error, but I am not an error. I am human and allowed to make mistakes, but I am not a mistake.

Only If

Is it time to end the burden of guilt when I accept that circumstance happen over which I have no control? Imagine, me not being able to control snow and rain that falls, temperatures that change into black ice on the highway! Imagine me not being able to control the car as it spins over the crest of a hill. Imagine me not being in control of the car and taking your life.
April 22, 1991

I read this letter at the Adult Children of Alcoholics class at Nativity Parish, where I truly started to heal. I needed to feel the pain, honor what I was feeling and give it all to God. It was the right idea, but not that easy to do.

Now that I had released my burden of guilt, I became more confident and decided it was time to place Hawaii on my goal list for the first time ever. It was now on my plan to be living on Maui by 2005. I would be living, or at least spending extended periods of time, on Hawaii.

I almost sabotaged my dreams of Hawaii once again. I used my bookkeeping skills to create a personal budget. What would it cost to move to Hawaii? How much would I have to save a month to make it there in ten years? What were my present living expenses? How much should I save for home repairs, property taxes? What should my savings be so I could take advantage of an IRA plan? Practical matters versus my heart's desire, a life-long choice for me.

I nearly questioned myself and my dream to death. By the time I got done with all the budgeting and savings questions, I was pretty sure Hawaii was out of the realm of possibility for those ten years, if not more. But, at least it was on my ten-year plan and that was a step forward. If I wanted to change my life again, I had to change my attitude and thought pattern. And

Only If

so I did. After all, "dreams are realities that are yet to be." And, dreams can come true only if…

Only If

The Decision

By the time 1991 rolled around, I was physically and emotionally depleted once again. I discovered the forty-six-year-old woman I had become was trying to relive and repair my early teenage years by caring for my employees. I was attempting to care for my siblings as I had done as a fourteen-year-old girl, trying to make it right a second time. It did not work out at forty-six or at fourteen or at seventeen when I left my father's home to live with his sister, escape the pain, do not allow myself to feel.

In October 1991, I closed a thriving business and just walked away. I just could not do it any longer. I figured I had failed yet again. I could no longer stand the pain in my life. Trying to keep control of everything sapped all my strength.

I finally got smart and decided to surrender it all to God. In February 1992, I started another business. I became an independent contractor as a part-time bookkeeper for dozens of clients. This time I had three employees: me, myself and God. My life started again as the Forensic Bookkeeper.

The following ten years were filled with discoveries and settling my life issues. I revisited my notes on all the self-help stuff over the years. I revisited my father's home again as a stranger would and found the same things a stranger would find who was not carrying my baggage. He had suffered a terrible loss. He had pain and guilt. He fought both sides of the family to keep his family together.

I went a step further and took a look at his family background through the eyes of a stranger. The Olson family was first generation farmers in the Kickapoo River Valley. The Olson boys worked from before dawn to well into the night. They farmed with horses and milked sixty head of cattle by hand. They provided for their family. In my grandfather's home, you had a roof over your head, clothes on your back, you went to church and the doctor and you were provided with a bounty of food laid before you at each meal. This is the love of the Olson family. To provide for your family was the way my father expressed his love to his motherless children. It was the only love he was capable to give. It was the love of his upbringing.

This was not the love I wanted as a fourteen-year-old child. I wanted hugs and kisses and snuggling, the way my mom's family did. I wanted to be listened to and talked with, not yelled at. I wanted to be able to ask for help and advice. I finally grew up and learned to honor the love my father expressed. It was not the love I longed for, but it was the best way he knew to express his love. Your physical needs were always met when my dad was around, and he was very good at providing for his family.

I came to realize my entire life had been filled with a succession of stumbling blocks or stepping-stones. Choices and decisions. Challenges and changes. My life changed daily. It was now time for me to take charge of the changes. I read self-help books, watched self-help programs. I removed toxic people from my life. I changed my lifestyle. I changed my thinking and I discovered peace and contentment, and a life filled with all the possibilities and no limits except those I placed upon myself. I made the choice to be happy.

Only If

Forgiveness is a wonderful thing. Peace is a wonderful thing. Integrity is a standard to bear proudly. Pride in who you are and what you do is to be honored. Forgiveness, peace, integrity, pride and self-esteem are all gifts you give yourself. They are self-bestowed. Only you can give them to yourself. Only you can take these away.

In the fall of 2000, my client, Wendy, asked me to attend a seminar by motivational speaker Anthony Robbins in Milwaukee, Wisconsin. Wendy, her husband and I traveled two hours to attend his learning seminar. Anthony reminded me to look for the good in any experience and not focus on the bad, only to learn from it. I learned to decide what my goals are and to focus on them. He reminded me that in order to change my life, I had to change my attitude, thoughts and actions. I walked away feeling empowered and courageous.

When 2001 rolled along, I had a sneaking suspicion this was going to be a year to be remembered. This year would be the most pivotal year of them all. Now I was in complete control of my life. I was responsible for my own feelings and allowed others the same privileges. I made the choices. I met the challenges. I grew and evolved. Or had I really been changing all along?

The week of March 19, 2001, was the one-year anniversary of my most recent visit to Hawaii. My son and I spent the better part of a two-hour phone conversation reminiscing on the three days we spent on Oahu and seven days on Maui in March of 2000.

For the past few weeks, I had been discussing Hawaii with Wendy. She was planning to attend an employee-training seminar in Wisconsin. I had encouraged her to sign up for the same one on Waikiki Beach on Oahu instead. Why not stay a few days more and go sightseeing? Why would anyone want to attend a seminar in the middle of winter in Wisconsin when you could do so on a tropical island? And a portion of the trip would even be tax deductible!

I had a feeling over the past few months that something was going to happen in my life. I had that little butterfly feeling in the pit of my stomach. It was not a fearful feeling, but one of expectation. I had this inkling of anticipation rolling around inside me and today was my day with Wendy, on her way to Hawaii. By the end of the day, I had made my decision.

After work, I met up with a friend, MJ. We went out for a light supper and a drink or two. By the time the evening was done, I shared my decision with her and she asked me, "What took you so long?"
Thoughts, plans and possibilities were racing through my head as I sat down at my computer. I prepared a letter to another friend, Joyce, who lives in England, and it read as follows:

March 19, 2001
Dear Joyce:

I came to a decision. Today was my day with Wendy, on her way to Hawaii. By the end of the day, I made my decision as well. Tonight MJ asked me to go for a light supper and a drink or two so she could talk to me about something. I let her have her time and then I shared my decision with her and now with you.

I have decided that life is too short to live in if only wondering.

I would rather be a has been than a never was.

I do not want to live in a world filled with regrets, as I have lived before.

Only If

Although I do not want to act in haste and repent in leisure, I too-often have lived in buyer's remorse by not getting something I desired or needed, and then have the opportunity pass me by and never be available to me again.

All the dreams I have ever imagined have come true, except two.

I have had only one intensive dream gnawing at me for forty years.

Only I am able to make it happen or let it pass me by.

I am articulate, accomplished, opinionated, and a worthwhile human being.

My greatest fault is that I make mistakes. My greatest attribute is that I learn from my mistakes. There is your time, my time, and God's time. I am on God's time and He is in control and peddling my bicycle.

I am moving to Hawaii.

Pick yourself up off the floor, dear Friend, grab a glass of wine and think about what you can do to make a living in your Paradise, or make one in New Mexico and visit me in my Paradise. This move will not be for at least six months for me because I have to save money to move there and keep my homes running in both places for a short time, but I am moving to Hawaii to see if living in Hawaii is for me or just too hot.

I have developed a plan of attack in the last 30 minutes and will type them up and send them to you. Let me know if I have missed anything, oh Thou of many moves! MJ wanted to know what took me so long to decide. Friends ... where would I be without them?

I wish only you and MJ to know of my plans right now. I will not tell anyone until I am further along. It is like when I was expecting Michelle after so many years and we did not tell anyone for a while just in case it did not happen yet again. Plus, my decision to move is my little secret to enjoy and ponder in privacy. More later.

Love, Linda

Only If

It is not as if this was an instant decision, for the love of Pete! I created the dream of living on a tropical island in 1959. The moment I set my foot on Maui in 1986, I knew Maui would be the tropical island of my fantasy. Now I will make it happen.

It was just that simple. Make a choice, make a decision, change your mind and change your life. By taking the leap of faith and making the decision, I found the creativity and energy to make it all happen.

On March 19, 2001, I decided the time had come. Now I will make it happen. It was just that simple. Make a choice, make a decision, change your mind and you will change your life. By making the decision and taking a huge leap of faith, I found the money, creativity and energy to make it all happen.

I spent the better part of the first week calling my accountant, the bank, and the IRS toll-free number to have some questions answered. What were the financial ramifications? How to proceed? Once I gathered the details and information, there was nothing left but to make it happen. I would call upon my Midwest work ethic and put my nose to the grindstone and just do it. Actually, putting my shoulder to the wheel and my back into my job seemed to be what was in store for me.

I needed to get the place in shape for my first goal: refinancing. FMHA homeowners have to reside on the property to keep the financing. We were still in the midst of winter in late March. Landscaping needs were out of the question for the time being, since the ground was covered with snow and the earth was frozen solid. I had no choice but to head into the basement, which I decided to call the bowels of hell. I had been working in the basement for only moments when the thought came to my mind that I would have rolled over in my grave if my adult son, Michael, had had to clean up this mess!

Although I put in five hours the first day, no one could really tell that I made any improvement in the basement whatsoever. Unless, of course, you looked out in the garage and saw the two bundles of cut-down and bound cardboard boxes, the five boxes filled with trash, and the three black trash bags bulging at the seams, just sitting there waiting for trash day. How does all this stuff accumulate?

Day two and I managed to put in another three hours on just the storage shelves on the outside of the spa room. My plastics recycling trash container, a 33-gallon monster on wheels, was filled to the brim. I managed another bundle of bound boxes as well.

After two hours, I set up a card table that I had already put out for the trash and sat down to organize six assorted boxes of nuts, bolts, nails, screws and repair items. It all managed to be packed easily into two old Tupperware containers I had not used for fourteen years. What a pack rat. Did I really think I needed all this stuff much, less would use it all? Girl Scouts may have taught me to be prepared, but this is overdoing it.

This dream of moving to Hawaii is the most dynamic dream I ever had. This was very complicated and required detailed attention. I had helped many people make their business dreams come true. Now, I would use all those organizational skills for me, giving me the best I had available for making my dreams comes true as well. Over all the years, I never got so much as a bonus for any businessperson I helped. Now, my bonus payoff would be Hawaii.

I seemed to become energized by the prospect of spring finally breaking the bitter cold of winter in Wisconsin. Of course, the excitement of working toward Hawaii pulled me through the first two weeks of sheer physical labor in the basement. After those two weeks, I realized I needed a little more research. All this stuff I had accumulated, all the money spent to purchase it, and for what good? There were tools, and the repair and maintenance stash in the basement. What would it cost to ship? Then there were the two bedrooms, the office and the living room and kitchen to think about. Of what real value was all this stuff, anyway?

I had a close personal relationship with the internet for a few days. It is amazing what you can learn over the internet. I found it would average $1.13 per pound to ship. How much does a loveseat weigh anyway? A chair and ottoman? Of course, I could use a 24-foot container for only $6,000! Good grief, all my stuff was not worth $6,000 to me. My first change plans to move to Hawaii was a drastic one.

My original plan was to keep the home in Wisconsin for a year and live in Hawaii for a year to test things out. I would explore the marketplace for my career; experience the cost of living; learn about the weather and how it mixed with my needs. If the weather was too hot or the job market soft or the prices too high, I could always come back to Wisconsin.

This decision just did not compute. The stress of wondering about the property in Wisconsin would be a drain on the energy I needed on Maui to grow my business again. I considered hiring a neighbor to look at my home each day for so much a month, but thought that to be an intrusion on her time and not a responsibility she should have at any price. If I am going after a dream, I have to have faith it will happen. I have to go all the way to commit to it.

Plan two: sell my home and my possessions, and move to Hawaii. Period. Make a commitment. Go for the gold. Anything that can be eroded by rain and wind had no real meaning for me anyway. They are only possessions and can be purchased anywhere. My personal relationships with those I love and those who love me were the real valuables I had. My love of nature, my eye for the tiniest of detail in each day, these valuables were portable. My sense of design was portable. My home was always carried within me. Let's go for the gold here!

When I look back and think about myself that first month, I sounded like Mr. Spock from *Star Trek* fame, "Linda, your decision to move to Hawaii, without a job, you don't know a soul, you have no place to live, no assets, and leave all you own behind, is totally illogical."

A lot he knows, he used to soar amongst the stars on the shirttails of someone else's dream. Why can't I? Surely I deserve the stratosphere at least! I made the decision to not tell my family and most people I knew until the last possible moment, because they might say the same things as Mr. Spock. I don't want a naysayer in my company these days. I know it will be a struggle to start a career all over again, but the rewards of living my dream environment will be worth it to me. A forty-year dream come true.

I remember all the times I procrastinated on setting goals as successful business people did. I thought I knew better than they did. Now I realize it is ever so simple to make decisions when I have clear-cut goals. Which choice will best get me to my goal? Will it move me toward the goal or away from it? The choices become so simple.

This was the first time I focused so intently on my goals. Other goals I had set had come true and just seemed to fall into place. This one would fall into place, too.

I revised another goal: By June 1st, 2001, I will have my home on the market to be sold.

Only If

By Thanksgiving Day, 2001, I would be in Hawaii, in my own place. That was that. "So be it," as my dad would say.

Only If

On The Market

I stripped the wallpaper off the bathroom walls, spackled and sanded spackle that "did not need sanding." I patched, painted, taped the trim and washed the paint that still somehow got on the trim. I discovered corners that had not been cleaned for a decade. Have you checked the tops of your kitchen cabinets lately? And when was the last time you moved your stove? Neither were pretty sights for me.

I hired a handyman to do the stuff I could not do. It came to just under $1,000, or 50 percent more than I thought it would and 25 percent more than I had saved. The faucet broke when he tried to take the old hoses off the washer that had rusted on over these fourteen years. Then, of course, the water main turnoff in the basement broke when he tried to turn off the water. I still giggle when I think of the look that must have appeared on his face when the turnoff valve broke off in his hand. The fan in the spa room stopped working so that got replaced. It was time, since it was thirteen years old. Then there was a drain clog that was 113 feet out. Fortunately, only wash water was backing up on my basement floor.

I was also "blessed" when high winds ripped through my little community, tore off part of the fascia board on the south side and blew shingles off the roof. Have you ever tried to replace only fifteen shingles that are fourteen years old? And let us not forget the three storm windows I had to repair. I took them to the shop, but when they were returning them to me, one blew off the truck and shattered. Thankfully, they gave me a new window from that event.

Then there were the endless hours of yard work. I make all these plans in October as part of goal setting, and then I have the entire summer to make it happen. Now I was going to complete the design on my 85-foot x 15-foot flowerbed in a matter of a few weeks.

For the first time in my life, I found a weed killer that really kills. Nary a blade of quack grass sprung to life where I used this wonder product! I hauled and spread eighteen bags of mulch and six 40-pound bags of topsoil. Kaukauna Floral and Stein Gardens and Gifts are surely considering opening a section and calling it "Linda's Folly in Flowerbed Maintenance." The stock boys all walked the other way when I came through their gates. They knew what I had in store for them three bags at a time.

I thought I would be smart and hire a professional to cut down two trees and trim the dogwood and Potentilla bushes. Bad move on my part. The tree stumps were still there after they left. They all started growing new suckers – an interesting choice of words now that I think about it. The dogwoods were not selectively trimmed of the dead wood and thick branches, as I had asked. They were pretty much butchered by a small circular saw! They were "trimmed" the first of April, and by mid-June, my bushes were just starting to fill out and not look so emaciated.

I put forth a lot of effort that spring. I completed all my tasks one day before the first day of summer. As of June 17, at 3:00 p.m., my tasks were done and I was ready to list my home with my real estate agent three days later. I missed my original target of June 1st by twenty days, but I made it. If all goes well, I will be having someone's idea of a traditional Thanksgiving Dinner in my new home on Maui.

Only If

I am sure there were those among my friends and family that thought me daft for such a move. "No, I have no place to move to, but I do know three areas where I would like to settle on Maui." "No, I have no job lined up. I researched the job market there. I am confident I can provide my bookkeeping services on Maui just as I do here. I made a niche for myself here and I can do the same there." "I have confidence in my abilities and the last time I looked, Maui was still in the USA!"

I know this is the right move for me. This has been a dream of mine for over forty years; now is the time to make it come true. If not now, when? I made the decision. I am making it happen. There will be no knight in shining armor coming to sweep me off to Maui. I have to make it happen.

Actually, all the little things that went awry were opportunities yet again for stumbling blocks or stepping stones, or just pure enjoyment of the moment. So I am glad the drain clogged and <u>only</u> laundry water went all over the floor. The clog was gone and I used this soapy water to wash the basement floor that recently had been cleared of trash and fourteen years of accumulated clutter.

So, the basement faucets broke. That allowed me to put new hoses on the washer and new faucets, too. The water in the village of Wrightstown is very hard, and the two metals had corroded together; not a good thing. The water main obviously needed replacement and now the new owner does not have to worry about it breaking and flooding their basement for another fourteen years. Rather have those things happen now than when someone is being shown my home. I would be mortified if someone walked into the basement and the floor was flooded.

Only If

Removing years of greasy film from under the stove saved me a great deal of personal embarrassment. I had no idea I had a problem until I moved the stove so I could touch-up the wall's paint. Have you removed your stove recently? I could not believe the mess. I am sorry to say I had not moved it since the day I moved in. Ick.

Once the tops of the kitchen cupboards were clean, I dressed them up with boughs of ivy and daisies. Little tendrils cascaded over the edges of the cupboards and tiny butterflies danced to the breeze of the ceiling fan. Charming – just like on HGTV or the show *Curb Appeal*, my mentors!
And I learned that my idea of how things should be done is not necessarily the same as the professional I may hire to do a job. So, the details are in the discussion of the task at hand. My wants and expectations need to be expressed and I cannot make an assumption on what a tradesperson will do. I need to ask, show and tell, get it in writing and check and comment on the work, before I write the check.

The greatest challenge before me in mid-June was to hoe the flowerbeds to deter any new little darling that may want to take over my thriving flowerbeds again. The riding lawn mower will be easy to use, and I can put up with that weed eater for one more summer. Only the house will pose the problem of keeping it tidy and ready for inspection. There seems to be ghosts who come in daily to mess up my home!

It is funny how many other opportunities can come my way when I am looking for the good things in every happenstance. When I used to walk through life expecting bad things to happen, they sure did. That is what I focused on. That is what I found.

For many years now, I have looked for the good things that happen in any event. Bad things happen to everybody in every day of life. By looking for the good, I find it. This new attitude provides many unexpected opportunities to come my way. There were many opportunities to grow, learn, laugh and live a better life each day.

On my way home from visiting my Aunt Sadie in Michigan, I decided to stop in Oconto, Wisconsin, to visit a friend, Pam. Since my home was on the market now, I started discussing my plans with my friends. Pam made a few calls and handed me some leads. I now had the names of two women who worked in the accounting departments of two major companies on Maui. Pam also called a contact she had in the last company she worked. He is approaching retirement age and sent me a book on the top companies in the islands, sort of a who's who directory of the business community.

A few days later, I shared my unfolding adventure with another long-term client. She gave me a lead to someone who knew someone who lives on Maui and may have a place for rent. Well, actually, he did not have a place for rent, but he was invaluable to me via e-mails with information on different parts of the island as I looked for a place to rent for a month. "Thank you, God, for putting my friends in my life."

I received nothing but positive feedback from the letter I wrote to everyone telling of putting my home on the market and moving to Maui. Members of the "Hat Ladies" group all responded with such positive statements, such as, "You go for it girlfriend" and "If only I had the guts" and "You are an inspiration." Their comments still give me goose bumps.

My sister, Lisa, sent me an e-mail saying she was "in awe and speechless." Another sister, Louise, wondered if my move was due to health problems the past fall. I told her that because of the health issue, I was able to become strong and healthy for the first time in my life.

Only If

My trip to Maui in 2000 was planned to show my son The Sacred Pools at the edge of the Pacific Ocean. This ancient lava flow cascades from the 10,023-foot peak of Haleakala Volcano. It is the spot I want my ashes scattered and I needed to share this place with my son. Only months before, I truly thought I was going to die. By the time the scheduled trip came up, I had a remarkable improvement in my health. I then used the trip to show my son the place of my dreams.

I realized on that trip that any days remaining in my life need to be spent fulfilling my dreams. I now had the energy to match the desire to move to Maui. Louise shared the reaction of my father. It was a hoot and nearly word-for-word what I expected. He asked her if she had gotten a letter from me about the move. "You know she's gonna take and move? What the hell she wanna go and move all the way to Hawaii for?"

Louise and I both had a good laughed over that one. I expected my dad's reaction. He is seventy-seven and has lived within 200 miles of his birthplace his entire life. He did take a trip to Wyoming to find one of his brothers, and for a lark he took a road trip to Florida. Louise told him it was a lifelong dream of mine. "And besides, she wants to retire there. Just because you want to be in the godforsaken winter doesn't mean she does!"

My mom's family in Madison and Goodman, Wisconsin, and Kingsford, Michigan, were all very proud of me. My aunt and I went to Kauai in 1991. Unknown to me at the time, Kauai was fulfilling a life-long dream for her, so she easily identified with my dream. My family of birth and those I have chosen to be my family have been 100 percent supportive. Mike, my son, was very happy for me and glad to have a place to crash when he visits Maui again. He, too, has fallen in love with Hawaii.

Only If

Now that the intense physical labor was complete, it was so nice to be able to focus on mental rather than physical stuff. I updated my resume so it was ready when I started working on my job searches. Then there was the temporary and long-term housing, and other leads I pulled from the *Maui News* using the internet.

There actually was an offer on my home after only two weeks on the market, but thankfully, it fell through; yet another opportunity for me. I would have had to close and move in thirty-four days. Too short for me! I had no clue on how to dispose of my stuff yet. I already called about extended stay hotels locally. They are $30 to $35 a day, or $990 a month. Too rich for my blood. On Maui, I was looking for a room to rent in a private home. There were many in the paper. Maybe I will just pack a pup tent – or buy one there. Don't have to worry about freezing at night at the ocean's edge on Maui!

My friends and family all knew I was not running away from anything. I was not running toward anything either. I was not making the move to Hawaii to become happy. I am a happy, content and successful woman moving to my idea of paradise. I was making a choice and did what it took to make a long-standing wish / dream of mine come true.

No one will step forward and take a magic wand and grant a wish for me; I need to grant it for myself. My forty-year dream was to live in Hawaii. If my life there lasts for twenty years, I will be very happy. If it is for twenty months, that's all right by me, too. If it is for ninety days, it will be an extended working vacation.

No matter what the future brings me, I cannot lose. I will be doing what I want and making my own choices to be happy, pleased, content, creative and energized! I now have my "horse before the cart" and we are traveling down life's highway, and I am holding the reins. Of course, God is the real driving force, but He lets me do the work most of the time.

I am very proud of what I have accomplished. If I ever tell anyone that I think I am a lazy person, I want them to just smack me upside the head, please! What I accomplished from March 19, 2001, to June 17, 2001, were not the actions of a lazy person. They were the actions of a motivated, energized "crazy person" working to make her dream come true.

Only If

The Reunion of Survivors

My dad is 77 at this time. He is a straight shooter. He is witty and has a snappy repartee when the opportunity presents itself. He is an independent thinker. He knows exactly what he wants. He does exactly what he wants and does not do what he does not want to do. I have lovingly called him an old fart for the better part of twenty years, and he loves to hear the name. A small smile curls his lips and he sort of snorts a laugh.

In 1997, dad had an eye removed due to cancer. It was the first time any of his five daughters had heard anything about cancer. Being the private person Dad is, he had not told any of us about his other bouts with cancer that started in 1993. There had been many visits and treatments in a doctor's office for polyps. In 1993, Dad had seven weeks and forty x-ray treatments for prostate cancer. The treatment worked and the cancer was eradicated. We also discovered his hearing loss and realized he did not completely understand what was happening at the doctors' visits. From 1997 to this day, one of my sisters goes with my father to all medical appointments. He may not want to bother anyone, but it more of a bother not to know his health needs.

Things seemed to be going well until January 7, 2000, when after a routine clinic visit, my dad discovered one carotid artery was completely blocked and the other was 95 percent blocked. He was at St. Mary's Hospital in Madison for surgery to open the right artery and restore blood flow to the brain. How does one walk around with only 5 percent of his blood flow working? This was the first priority of surgery.

On January 31, 2000, again after a routine follow-up visit for his surgery, they found a mass in the colon region that required removing the right sphere of his colon. As part of pre-operation procedures, the doctors received consent to remove any other organs that were affected or impaired. Good thing, too. During the operation, the doctors noticed his gall bladder was full of stones, so that was removed as well.

Dad was a man that generally never complained about any health problems. He told the doctor the gall bladder never bothered him, and in fact, he "had no idea he even had a gall bladder" let alone what it was for.

Six days after surgery – only hours after getting home – he was rushed back to St. Mary's to have a bile leak repaired. The leak was a result of a missed stitch by the residents that finished the procedure, a very common mistake or oversight. Dad had to remain in the hospital in critical condition due to the amount of bile in his system. He was on antibiotics for ten days and the doctors told my sisters not to take this lightly. Dad was very sick. His cavity had been filling with bile since the day of surgery. He was on pain medications and did not know he had a problem until the meds wore off once he got home.

Dad was not able to bounce back very quickly from those surgeries. A six- to eight-week recovery stretched into ten to twelve weeks.

Dad was just feeling really good in May when he had to face diverticulosis in June. The doctors and nursing staff were always amazed at how quickly Dad would bounce back. The stubborn Norwegian and Irish stock stood him in good stead through these health trials. Dad had been going in for regular blood tests to check for cancer markers that were only slightly elevated.

In December of 2000, they performed a rectal exam because he was experiencing discomfort in his bottom. Dad told my sister, Louise, that they had found a mass in the rectum. They removed the colon the following January, closed the rectum and Dad now had a colostomy bag. The man was remarkable yet again. He regained his strength, but not quite as fast as before.

His attitude was so great. He told me, "You learn to live with a bag if it is the only way you can live." He has such a great attitude. He is amazing. He always made jokes about the bag, but it was just to cover his self-consciousness about it making any noises and the possibility of leaks.

After his most recent hospital stay, I told him, "You are obnoxious, ornery, cantankerous and bullheaded. And those are your good characteristics." You have to fight fire with fire with my dad. It was my way of a pep talk. He had recovered from all the others. He would recover from this one. It is just that at 77, not even he could expect to hop out of bed in 24 hours and go home. This last surgery was more complicated and would require more time to recover. Not that any of his cancer treatments over the past seven years had been easy.

That February in one of our weekly phone conversations, I gave him my speech again and told him he would be fine by St. Patrick's Day (March 17). And he was. But it sure took a lot out of him this time.

My sisters live near my dad and have given him all the physical and emotional support one could ask for. He had his apartment and they would bring him leftovers and hot meals, and make phone calls and short visits here and there. He kept a six-pack of Milwaukee's Best beer chilled in the refrigerator just for Louise. He wants the visits short so his illness does not interfere in our lives. My sisters are the care providers. All I can do is call and write my long letters.

Since his surgery in January 2001, he began to talk a lot to Louise about his youth on the farm in the Kickapoo River Valley, Gays Mills and Soldiers Grove, Wisconsin – his boyhood stomping grounds. He chatted about the weather and doing most of the farm chores with horses. The brothers and sisters and the games they played. The trouble they got into as they grew up. Louise got in contact with two of his brothers to let them know of Dad's health. She would periodically drop a note to keep them up to date, but we suggested they not contact Dad. My dad is pretty stubborn, but sensitive and a private person, and does not like to be fussed over.

I don't remember how it actually happened, and Louise was the main driving force, but over a couple months, a plan was hatched. We were talking to Dad's brothers behind his back. We knew he would have wanted his illness to be private, but we thought it should be shared if only for health history.

Our plan was to have our "Third Annual Olson Girls Get Together" at Louise's again, slated for July 21, 2001. Only this time, there would be two unexpected guests, two of his three remaining brothers. These are the last four of a family of eleven children. And we were going to get them together for the first time since 1991, the funeral of his last surviving sister, our Aunt Dettie.

So the long-established roles of life had now been reversed. Instead of Dad relishing his Santa Claus days when we were kids and keeping secrets from us, we were keeping secrets from him. His daughters were relishing their thoughts instead. It would be our Mrs. Santa Claus experience for our dad. His present would be a surprise reunion.

I had long ago solved issues about my dad. I elected not to share my feelings of bitterness, loss, resentment, and being forces to raise his kids. They were my thoughts, feelings and interpretation of my life experiences from my point of view. His point of view and views of a total stranger would not match my views. I put the feelings in the past, where they belong. I chose to be happy. I am so happy I did this, especially based on his years of health issues. I did not need to burden his soul as well.

Dad kept his regular quarterly doctor's appointment the first part of July. He got another clean bill of health from the lab tests. There were a couple spots on his lungs, but they had been there for years and had never changed. One spot was a little larger now, though. However, the readings from his CAT scan were not to be read until July 24 and he would see his cancer doctor for the results. Dad had already said if they found something, he did not want to be unzipped again. Three times in one spot is enough for him.

But he did say that last time as well. How much can one person be expected to take? How much control should he have over his life? I am sure glad the surprise party was for July 21, before he goes to the doctor.

Dad was told about the family cookout and that I was coming from Green Bay. But he did not know his brother, Lawrence, from Mequon, Wisconsin, and Buddy, from La Crescent, Minnesota, would be coming. One brother was in Colorado – unreachable by choice, he is an independent Olson to the end, after all. Buddy's wife is dealing with ovarian cancer, so she may not make the trip. We did tell Buddy about this newest office visit so a better-informed decision could be made. It would just be a few hours' trip from La Crosse to Blue Mounds and might be the last time for Buddy to see my father alive.

One of the lessons I learned in my life has served me well over the years. That lesson is to not have unrealistic expectations of any event. By taking that attitude, I allow myself to achieve the fullness of any experience. And so it was this July 21, 2001.

Louise and I got up at 6 a.m. that Saturday and enjoyed a pot of coffee on her deck. The morning air was already thick with humidity, but very enjoyable for that hour in the early morning coolness of the day. The robins and mourning doves were almost annoying in the loudness of their chatter. Almost, but not quite. She has a lovely setting and a mature flower garden. The lots are larger than one would expect at a trailer, and it all makes for a very nice place to raise a child. The neighbors were kind, friendly and thoughtful. Everyone seems to take care of his or her property. She had a nice community to live in.

The sisters starting calling at 8 a.m., checking in for the day and seeing if anything more was needed on their way to Louise's home. Louise went out about 9 a.m. to put out green balloons and "Olson" directional cards at key turning spots for the brothers to follow. She was hoping Dad would not take the scenic route to her home and notice the Olson name on the signs.

The sisters arrived at 9:30 and 10:00, and dad shortly thereafter. After hugs and hellos, we went into the air-conditioned trailer. There was the chatter and banter and stories to share. Soon, a comfortable familiarity came over the six of us for the next hour. We were all together again, in one spot. This was the first time since my daughter's death in 1984. It was such a nice feeling and another memory I will forever cherish.

Only If

Along about 11 a.m., Dad decided to set up the sprinkler. He got his granddaughter, Lindsay, this elephant-shaped water sprinkler. Dad, forever the farmer/gardener, found a creative way to do the watering job plus invite and give permission for Lindsay and her pals to get refreshed as the grass and gardens become watered. My son, Mike, called to say he was on his way.

Then someone said a car was coming. I told Mike I would have to call him back because "the brothers are here!"

The first woman out of the car looked like my Aunt Joan, but still in her forties. Uncle Buddy and his wife and daughter were introducing each other to my sisters. After my hug from Uncle Buddy, I went to the back yard to get Dad from his sprinkler duty. I told him to come up front; we had something to show him. The two brothers came around their respective sides of the tree and saw each other for the first time in nine years.

There were smiles and warm handshakes and hugs with Dad and Buddy. He introduced his wife and daughter. Tammy looks just like the Joan I remembered from decades ago, and I told here so. I can still see Buddy and Joan and the two young girls sitting on a blanket under the big oak tree in Grandma Olson's yard twenty-five or thirty years ago. I could almost hear the rushing waters of the brook and feel the winds blowing down from the tall limestone bluffs. It was such a deja vu experience for me.

We decided it was way too warm outside, so we headed for the air-conditioned trailer. I was picking up the rear when another car pulled up and Uncle Lawrence arrived. I greeted those two and escorted them into the house. Due to the confusing nature of now ten people in the house and two more popping in, I was not privy to Dad, Buddy and Lawrence's first meeting together. It was so wonderful to see them together in one room for something other than saying goodbye to another brother or sister.

Only If

Before long, the burgers and brats were on the grill. I helped the sisters set up the buffet line in the kitchen. Louise fixed Dad's plate, and I got Buddy and Lawrence to the line and the other sisters kept the rest busy with beverages and conversation.

Everything went so smoothly. The hot food was hot and the cold food was cold, and the spicy food was SPICY! Leeanna made her cold taco salad that is always such a hit. I am such a pansy when it comes to spicy foods. I am the only one in the family who does not like spicy food. Uncle Buddy even put some jalapeno rings on his food by the spoonful. They are all true, hot-blooded Olsons. My son does love the hot stuff, so he makes up for me.

Another Olson characteristic came out, and I don't know what I was thinking of. I expected these older people to sip diet soda and water. Wrong!

Beers all around with the meal, only Dad had bottled water. I made some comment about being surprised you boys were drinking beer. Uncle Buddy said, "We are Olson boys after all!" Of course, I forgot all the stories about the boys growing up. I thought of them being elderly and surprised they were drinking at all, but did not share my thinking pattern.

Uncle Buddy was always my favorite. I had a crush on him from an early age and he still looked handsome and charming to me. At the Olson funerals and weddings, I always sat with Lawrence and Barb, so I was very comfortable with them, too. Barb is still beautiful and charming and looked the same today as she did the past twenty years.

Buddy's daughter, Tammy, is a kick. The girls really like her and I do hope they get together periodically. I did not have as much time with Tammy as two of my sisters and Mike did. They were the smoking contingent and had conversations outside in the humid smoking room deck. They seemed to hit it off well, too.

Only If

The brothers sat at the dining room table and chatted from noon until about 5 p.m. Each of us took our turn eavesdropping at the table and hearing a story or two. We all filtered from the deck to the living room to the dining room table. This was just what we wanted, the three of them getting together and sharing memories and laughter, each sister getting a chance to chat and share, and then move on to the wives. Nothing was planned; it all unfolded that way. It was beautiful and filled with grace.

We all expected Dad to head out by 3 p.m. at the latest. He just hung in there, yakking away. Tammy called her husband to let him know they, too, were staying longer than expected. Things were just going so well. Tammy reminded Buddy that he had promised to take videos of the day, and he charged out to the sweltering car to get the video camera. Barb remembered her Polaroid and got that as well.

We laughed our heads off at Buddy, Lawrence, Louise and several other people trying to operate the video camera. Someone asked, "And how many Norwegian Olsons does it take to operate a video camera?" and everyone laughed. Louise was taking a video of him taking a video of her. People were snapping photos here and there. What a hoot!

Somewhere in the midst of all this, my move to Maui came up. I shared my fantasy of being on a Maui beach, reclining in a lounge chair under an umbrella, gazing at the island of Lanai. Several hard-bodied men doing the hula would surround me cater to my every need – for drinks, of course! I told them my cell phone and laptop were nearby, and when the phone rang I would say, "Thank you for calling the Bookkeeping Lady. What credit card will you be using today?"

Everyone was into my fantasy, hooting and making comments. I then noticed Buddy's video camera on the table and the red light was on. I said,

"Oh, my God. He has the camera on!" I left the room to rolling laughter by everyone, including me. What an experience. I did tell Uncle Buddy, however, I would not pay blackmail.

About 5 p.m., we began to pose for photos with several people taking pictures with the cameras of people in the pictures. Barb's Polaroids came out really well. Louise took temporary possession to make copies on her computer for all of us. Everyone had hugs and handshakes, and it took about twenty minutes just to say goodbye. Buddy and his family were the first to go.

Louise, Leeanna, Leslie and Lisa were on the deck and the lawn, waving their arms to Tammy, and they were all yelling "goodbye" back and forth with everyone laughing. I walked with Dad arm and arm to his car and pointed his attention to his daughters on the deck and lawn yelling goodbyes to all.

I said, "Look at your daughters. They are all crazy aren't they?" He said, "Yes, they are." There was a catch in his throat and his eyes were misty. Dad left then, and Lawrence soon after.

The day was more than anyone could have asked or prayed for. The brothers were so glad to see each other. Everyone got on so well. Dad did not leave early as we completely expected. He was not mad, which was a treat to us all because none of us were sure how he would react to our surprise. The food was very good and there was enough for everyone. The air conditioning saved the ninety-five degree day.

There are not enough superlatives to describe what our experiences were. Each of our emotions was different based on our life's experiences and what we saw. We needed to get together and share our personal experiences so we could expand the day's events even further.

Only If

We all have a happy memory filled with laughter and tears, photos and attachments, some renewed and some made for the first time. It was a great day in the Olson family; a day of survivors of life. We all survived whatever life has thrown our way.

Forty-two years ago, our mother had died in an auto accident. My father lost the love of his life, his soul mate. He was left alone with six kids to care for ranging in age from three weeks to me at thirteen. We were a tremendous responsibility for a man to care for. In 1977, he lost his only son. In 1984, he lost his grandchild.

As children, we could offer no support, only a burden. Now, as adult women, his daughters all came together to support our father and help make a wish come true for him, to spend a few more hours in his youth with his brothers.

No matter where I go or what I do, I will always remember that Saturday with the uncles, aunts and cousins, and a Saturday early evening with my sisters. With the Olson men having left, only the sisters and my son remained. I had created a box for each of them as I packed and sorted my personal possessions. I gave out a few things I had treasured over the years. I had saved all the greeting cards, colored pictures from my nieces and nephews, and school and family photos. I returned Leeanna's First Communion veil she had given me. I gave Mike his baby book and the gown he and his sister were baptized in, among other things.

I had craft things I made that I did not want to trash, and craft supplies I was not taking to Maui. These little things were special to me or something I knew was special to them. They were given unconditionally with no expectations they would use, keep or fall in love with. No strings attached.

Only If

    Leeanna got out her great photo albums she put together of her family and some of all of us. Mike dug out my albums he had so I could take them with me to my new home on Maui. We had a great time talking, laughing, reminiscing and creating new memories as the sun was setting on this most blessed of days.

    Thank you, God, for this day, for such a special time with my family; for sharing of old memories and for the making of many new memories; for the reunion of three of the four remaining Olson brothers. To have none such a day that has ever been before or we will ever see again, to make a dream come true for our dad.

Only If

The Estate Sale

One more hurdle to cross. I had a pretty good idea what I was taking with me and what I was giving away. Now, how do I get rid of the rest of it?

Ask and it will be answered.

In stepped another of my friends, Sheila. We have known each other since 1977, and if ever anyone should have the bumper sticker "This Car Stops At All Garage Sales", it would be Sheila's car, Betsy. This veteran of many a garage sale, an experienced shopper and negotiator, made me the offer to help me put on a garage sale. Being the smart person I am, I took her up on the offer, except we would call it an "Estate Sale" at my home on August 18, 2001.

The week before the sale, Sheila came to my home that soon would become just a house again. And so the disassembly of my home began. Tables were set up. Things taken off the walls, out of cupboards, out of drawers, and all marked with stickers I had created on my computer the week before. We put signs on the walls and instructions on the doors to control the traffic flow. I was so out of my element. I had never had a sale before, but I had put myself in the hands of a master.

We ended the day sitting at two card tables in the living room. Dear, sweet, Sheila had brought along lime green poster boards, felt-tip pens and block lettering. We began making a dozen huge signs to tell of the estate sale.

Only If

Sign after sign was completed. We stapled, nailed and taped them to tomato steaks I would no long need. I had a brilliant idea and collected some of my orange tiger lilies and stapled them to a corner or two of each. Lime green and orange. A person would have to be color blind not to see these!

And so, it began. The estate sale went well, very well indeed. I have never had one before and don't plan to have another one again, thank you very much! After the sale, my life as it used to be had been condensed to about five boxes of things and stuff that could be picked up by a local thrift shop that supports a home for unwed mothers.

Never having had a garage sale before, I had been told of what to expect. "If you advertise it to start at 9 a.m., they will still come at 7 a.m." Everyone was right. I even had someone stop in on Friday afternoon. I had the garage door opened about 12 inches and I heard a rap on the door. A lady would not be able to attend on Saturday, asking if she could, "Please look so my daughter can come and buy something for me if I want it?"

Dumbfounded, I let her in. True to her word, her daughter did come back and get quite a bit of stuff. Go figure!

People came pouring in at a steady stream on Saturday morning. Judy and Eileen live on my block and knew most of the people that attended. They made everyone feel comfortable and asked for special pricing from Sheila or me when necessary. These two long-term residents of Wrightstown greeted relatives, neighbors and strangers as they came into my home. They kept the traffic pattern going and mentioned my impending move. "She can't take it with her, so no reasonable offer will be refused."

In the early afternoon, a young lady came walking to me at the cash box (my assigned location by Sheila) carrying the "Sacred Blender." My friend MJ and I looked at each other and said, "Margarita."

Only If

Our "Sacred Blender" for our Hat Ladies gatherings was sold to a college student going to the University of Wisconsin-Stevens Point in the fall. She needed something to make margaritas in the dorm! It not only went to a good home, but also it would be attending college!

And so did the stories MJ and I related to this young girl and her mom about the traditions of the "Sacred Blender and the Hat Ladies" that needed to be upheld. I escorted this young girl, arm and arm, to the kitchen counter and the assortment of margarita glasses, and asked her to pick one free of charge, use it and think of the Hat Ladies. I will be known far and wide as the "crazy old lady on Janet Court" after the experiences of the estate sale.

It was such a wonderful experience. I saw nameless faces from church, the grocery store, gas stations and a few eating places. I had a chance to meet many of the people that purchased items. We exchanged stories on the history or experience of the goods, and they shared with me why they have a need or how it will be used in their life.

The 29-inch television would be used to give the girls their own area in a rec room. Sports are big in Wisconsin, but not all members of this family were Green Bay Packers fans (poor things).

The three retro 1950's rust fabric and chrome side chairs went with the rust and orange braided rug from the summer porch to two young men setting up an apartment together. It is good to know that most of my wordily goods went to good people who will enjoy their purchases.

My sets of dinnerware went to two wonderful homes. A college student purchased the black set to bring to the apartment he is sharing with some other guys. This stoneware should last a long time. He also purchased a few pots and pans under his mother's guidance.

Only If

A young couple, moving in together, purchased the fancy dinner set my aunt gave me for Christmas one year. She did not want it back, so I sold it. There was a matching coffee serving pot, sugar, creamer and gravy boat, plus the service for eight. It was my first-ever matching set. I drastically reduced the black stem wine glasses to go with the set, and tossed in the black dinner napkins with the white rings to complete the dining experience. I told them how I always used linen napkins when I raised my kids. Paper napkins were for fishing or barbeques, not family meals.

MJ demonstrated and explained the fine art of packing dishes as she boxed up the set. When the young man came to pay me, I said wrapping dishes in paper was a good idea, but if one wants to avoid dirty dishes needing to be wash, he should pack the items in sheets and towels. Then the dishes are clean from one cupboard to another and protected. All you need to do then is fold up the linens that needed to be moved anyway! They were a cute couple.

Sheila had helped me organize, mark items, arrange tables, construct the signs and helped with sales. I still say her signs and organization played the largest part in the success of the sale. MJ, with a long-standing history of garage sales, was the ringmaster.

One young lady came to the estate sale a little saddened that someone had died and we were selling all her personal possessions.
"Died?" said MJ. "Hell, she's selling her stuff and moving to Hawaii! Don't feel sorry for her, feel sorry for us who are left behind!" The girl felt better after that.

These fine ladies and good friends rose to the occasion at every turn. They greeted people, directed them through the house and out of restricted areas; mentioned various stuff for suggestive selling, and then moved and condensed and relocated the items that were left for sale. What a job each one of them did, and I thank them all from the bottom of my itchy little feet. One of the secrets to a successful sale are the friends you have to help you. Not only do they do a fine job, but also they purchase a lot of your stuff.

After we had finished our little luncheon, I cleaned up the kitchen had them all come back into my kitchen.

"Look," I said. "This is the first time this counter has been bare since 1987!" It is easy to keep things clean when you have no more stuff. Most all of it went. Bags and boxes and arms full of my material "wealth" walked out of my life into the lives of my neighbors and unknown strangers that Saturday. The rain started about 4 p.m. and we were all very thankful to end the sale.

After we shut down, we all gathered in the empty living room. MJ gave me a package to open. Diane had created a family photo of me and my two children. A short time ago, I asked Diane, another Hat Lady, to see if she could do something for me. The spring after Michelle died, I had a church photo taken of Mike and me. Diane took the 8 x 10 and placed Michelle's eighth-grade photo in it on a beautiful blue background.

Diane had prepared another 8 x 10 for me with a sunset as the backdrop. Sheila could not hold back the tears and I was sort of in shock. I just did not think Diane would be done so quickly and never anticipated the beauty of it all. I called Diane to thank her for her loving kindness. I had to slip into the bedroom after the call to compose myself.

She was able to use her computer skills to give me the only photo I have of my two beautiful children and me together. No one can know what that means to me. One never really does know what we have until we lose it or when our time will come to leave this earth.

Only If

Diane gave both of my kids back to me that day. I even have a photo for my wallet. Thank you, Diane, for your act of kindness and using your skills and your heart to make another dream come true for me. It is so important to share your dreams with those you love and trust. Your loved ones can help you make your dreams come true.

Sunday morning, Sheila and I had our cereal in plastic food storage containers. Sheila, fortified by coffee and aspirin for her pain, suggested we open the garage doors and see what might happen. So I took the black magic marker and made several signs to tape to the road signs placed on a dozen corners that said "Sunday 9-1." I timed it to be seen before church in case anyone wanted to stop by.

I told everyone that came to make me a fair offer and I would probably sell it to them for less. And I did. Sheila kept adding to the box of free stuff. Three ring binders, office trays, and some sewing lace were chosen. Frayed towels and worn blankets I was going to toss out were taken for cleaning rags and a dog blanket. My boxes and boxes of canning jars found a good home for $5 and the pressure cooker canner went for $20. I hated to see that go at any price!

A 70-year-old widower came to my sale on a bike. He offered me a place to come and stay when I grow tired of the year-around summer weather on Hawaii. I can stay with him when I want to enjoy a Wisconsin winter again.

I patted him on the back and told him I might consider it since he was sensitive enough to appreciate and purchase all my tiger lily floral and wreath arrangements for his living room. I tossed in a 72-inch round dresser scarf, and he left with a smile on his face and my heart was so full.

Only If

Sheila and I sat one last time in the lawn chairs and spent a few moments together before she headed home. This was the last time to listen to the waterfall in the pond. The last time to admire the array of flourishing flowers in my garden. The last time together to see the purple finches, hummingbirds, and monarch butterflies, and hear the robins calling and the coo-coo-coo of the mourning doves. It was the last time to feel the summer breeze together after twenty-four years of friendship.

All the moments and times and hours we have spent together. All the memories and tears. All the belly laughs and giggles. Watching our kids grow up. Dealing with our divorces and the death of my daughter. All the experiences of a lifetime were felt this last day together. We said our tearful goodbyes and then she was gone.

I stayed opened one last hour alone and closed the garage door at 1:30 that Sunday. I took twenty minutes to tour the town and remove the estate sale signs. I went to the grocery and convenience stores and removed the signs for, "I can't take it with me to Hawaii so you might as well take it home." Sure did get a lot of great comments on all our signs.

I walked through the nearly-empty rooms. All vestiges of color, contrast, design and warmth were now adorning someone else's home. All that remained were two toss pillows and a partial box of books in the living room, and two pieces of artwork and the entertainment center for Michael. The dining room had the singer machine to be picked up next week and Mike's new dining set. Mike's old bedroom held the suitcases and boxes to be packed for Hawaii.

My office and bedroom were still complete. I was thankful for some semblance of order yet in at least one room. I need the office for my work and records to sort. Thanks go to Pam for letting me use some of the items she had purchased. I still had a bed to sleep on, and a rocker and the file cabinet. A few decorations I had created for my bedroom and the bed linens were not put up for sale. I had decided the week before to ship them to Hawaii. I only sold the containers the craft items were displayed in.

I had the same feelings about the collection of sunrises and sunset pictures. I took them out of the frames and placed the photos and art in a Tupperware box for my suitcase. So much of my dreams of Hawaii came from photos and pictures. The tangerine sheer curtains from my aunt had witnessed our many conversations in her living room, and then were part of my dreams of Hawaii when they were given to me. I had my living room in sunset colors of orange, tangerine and pale yellow accents against cream color walls.

The sunrise and sunsets, and endless hours of thinking and dreaming in my living room and bedroom were where I set my goals and dreamed my dreams. They all just had to come with me, and so they would. I would replace all the frames. Thanks to the sale, I had some extra money to do that.

I planned to ship my computer to Hawaii via FedEx, and a box or two of bedroom linens and flowers. I packed three suitcases and did much practice packing to pare down, but I had a month or two to simplify my life even more.

The ever-brilliant Sheila had me contact my real estate agent and get some fact sheets on my home. We had them at the cash box during the sale and handed them out as needed. Nine couples were shown through my home on that Saturday alone. MJ and Sheila did most of the touring, and shared stories and experiences they had in my home.

While preparing supper that Sunday night, I went into the living room to turn on PBS since my television from the kitchen counter was gone. I could not find the remote control. The end table I usually placed it on was gone. I looked on the half-wall between the rooms, but only my devil's ivy was there. I looked on top of the entertainment center and it was not there either. Then I wondered if I put it on top of the television for some strange reason. When I opened the entertainment center, the remote was not there and neither was the television. Dah! The mind is a terrible thing to waste.

One of the great experiences I have had I call the better part of dying. I am settling my own estate, if you will. I am tossing out things of no value or of no use to anyone, or revealing old memories that need not be shared. I am giving away most of my clothing to the YWCA for women who are entering the work place and in need of professional clothing. Wisconsin clothing will be too warm for the tropics.

The life I had in Wisconsin for the past fifty-six years was dying away day-by-day. I was giving back and passing along things of importance, and letting each person know what their gifts and their persona has meant to me. I had the rare privilege of dispensing my worldly goods to old friends, family, and new friends I met at my estate sale. The money from the sale gave me a good start for my furnishings in my rental home on Maui, Hawaii.

I was exiting my old life and continuing to open my being to all the possibilities my new life on Hawaii would have for me. I was open, creative, and imaginative, making no judgments or having no preconceived notions. I had the best of all possible worlds this day. I was excited, blessed, fulfilled, and quite exhausted.

The most wonderful part is my ability to dream and use my imagination again. I had lost that for many, many years after Michelle died. I lost my ability for "Dr. Schuller's Possibility Thinking" for my personal life. I kept that skill for my business life, for my customers, but could not imagine anything for me, for my life. For so many years, I was burdened with guilt and remorse. I created a life based on what I thought I deserved.

I remember one of the visions I had in one of my goal-setting sessions a few years ago. I was in a room with no walls, no ceiling, and no floor. It was all white. I had the physical floor for support under me, but there were no boundaries visible. I thought for a long time to understand that one. I came to realize that my life is a clean slate, an empty canvas if you will, to design the life I wanted for me. The life God wanted for me.

It is so wonderful to have the world back again at my fingertips, right there in my mind's eye. Like I told MJ recently, I have my boundaries, but my life has no limits. She told me to write it down so I don't forget it, and I did. I even remembered it without looking it up!

The only limits any of us have in our lives are the limits we impose on ourselves. Or those limits we allow others to impose upon us.

Only If

Letting Go and Saying Goodbye

As the hot and humid days of August passed, I still had a few corners here and there to clean out. The filing cabinets and boxes of old bank and tax records were sorted, some saved and some tossed. I still had some stuff in the basement that was not fit to sell or contribute for that matter, just tossing. So, I kept on doing a little here and a little there, bit by bit.

There were two corners to clean out that were seventeen years old. Two more bridges to cross. I finally went through the suitcase I packed in 1984 with mementoes of Michelle. I unearthed it the second day I started to clean the basement. I just sat it on the spa shelf, waiting for the moment when I was ready to open it. I was not uncomfortable with the prospect; I was only waiting for the right moment. The moment arrived on a Friday evening.

I had some CDs playing in my office as I was sorting. I spotted Michelle's suitcase on one of the trips downstairs to wash yet another load of clothes. I carried the suitcase upstairs and placed it on my desk. It was more than a little musty from fourteen years in my basement. I have always known just where it was when the moment came. I had not opened it since it was packed in 1984.

Only If

It was actually very wonderful to open it up and explore all the little things that are of great importance to a thirteen-year-old just entering Lombardi Junior High School in Green Bay. The first thing I opened was the envelope containing the jaw of a squirrel. Dad and Michelle took a walk in the woods on that Holy Saturday afternoon. Dad was always looking down to collect four-leaf clovers and came back with a few. Michelle was always curious about nature, found the jaw but presented me with a nosegay of lavender forget-me-nots. I imagine they discovered the jaw together and shared this special secret. I found the squirrel jaw in Michelle's pillowcase after returning from her funeral. She had died with her head on that pillow.

Mike and I went to the bereavement classes at Bellin Hospital about five months after Michelle died. On the last day of the class, the adults and children were separated and we each were asked to bring a show and tell item about the person who died. To this day I don't know what Michael took or I have forgotten.

I took the 8 x 10 color school photo of both Michelle and Michael, and the squirrel jaw. I said although I had lost Michelle, I would always have two children. One is in heaven now, but each are always in my heart and my soul. The jaw of the squirrel symbolized the joy and interest Michelle had for nature and for life. She had an inquisitive mind. I told them I imagined my dad and my daughter had a special time together the day before she died. Now, fourteen years later, I found comfort and joy in their making a memory the day before she died. I found some forget-me-not flowers and had placed them inside her photo frame.

Another corner of the suitcase contained the sympathy cards bound in red ribbon. Michelle's girlfriends gave them to me when she died. There was the note from the Girl Scouts troop I had led. They gave it to me with a decorative wreath the Scouts made for me and delivered the week I got back home from the funeral. The wreath has always been on display. I did not know what to do with the wreath. I could not toss it or sell it. One day Sheila's daughter, Michelle, admired it. I told her the story and asked if she would like to have it. She did. They were great friends as children. I was very thankful when Michelle admired it and I could give it to a family member.

I collected all my daughter's favorite reading books and gave them to my niece, Lindsay. I had a stash of stuffed animals that were still in the original bags I gave to two of my aunt's great-granddaughters, Serria and Mickala. The other stuffed animals and two dolls were beyond salvage and discarded.

I looked through the autograph book the school provided the class as they passed into junior high. What crazy little things they wrote to one another. Much the same silliness I wrote and received when I graduated eighth grade. I have her report cards, photos that were taken at Lombardi Junior High that January for being the most improved student in school. Once we figured she was dyslexic, there was no stopping her.

And there were many more special things. Things that broke my heart as I was packing them in April of 1984 now warmed my soul. I passed along to her dad the Bible he gave Michelle for Christmas 1983. I gave it to Michael with him having first dibs. If he did not want it, he should pass it on to his dad. I pointed out the letter Michelle wrote to her cat, Isaac, the night before we drove to my sister's for Easter dinner. Michelle hated to leave Isaac behind, so she wrote a letter to her cat and stuck it in her Bible.

That letter did bring a tear to my eye. I can still see my beautiful brown-haired Michelle, sitting Indian-style in her yellow and green canopy bed, and me telling her to stop writing the letter and go to sleep. Many items came with me to Maui. These are the only tangible things I have. It is silly, I know, but it is my right.

As the weeks progressed, I got more and more used to minimalist living. There was no clutter anymore, nothing to clutter on, nothing to clutter with, less and less to clutter my mind, only peace to free my soul. And yet, I missed none of all the tangible assets that were now gone. There is such joy in knowing I always have my valuables with me, carried in my heart and soul.

I carry within me my work ethics and my values. I carry my thoughts and my memories. I carry my love from the ones I love. I send the love I have back to them. These are the true essentials of my life. Those I love and those who love me are with me always, no matter how many miles or years separate us.

The next night, Saturday, I had another therapeutic experience. I had one more package I had to go through. I kept this package in my bottom desk drawer. I kept all the sympathy cards and guest book from Michelle's funeral in my desk all these years. I decided it was time to cross this one last bridge.

I had no preconceived notions on what I would feel. I was, however, surprised at how very uplifting and wonderful this experience was, too. I had no recollection of any of these cards. I worked for years and years to block every experience from those days and years out of my mind. I know I read the cards at one time, for I recognized my handwriting on the insides of some of the cards. I wanted everyone to know who these cards were from, so I asked family and Larry to write what relationship these people were to any one of us.

I read each and every one of the cards again with new eyes. The verses were now comforting and full of grace and wisdoms instead of the pain and grief, or guilt or lack of any feelings I may have allowed myself to have in April of 1984. There were even three cards and letters from strangers who saw the article on Michelle in the newspaper and wanted to offer some comfort to her family.

The thing that shocked me most of all was my realization of how many people were in my life all those years ago. Since the death of my mother in 1959, I lived in the world feeling lost, alone and unloved. But most shocking was the realization I was loved. This huge feeling of love and compassion came over me as I read those bereavement cards and personal notes. I had goose flesh on my arms. I finally realized I had always had family and friends who loved me. I had always had people who cared about me. The exile I felt was self-imposed.

Long ago I realized there is your time, my time, and God's time. The secret is to become part of God's time frame. I am saddened by the realization of all those years I had wasted reinforcing the pain of guilt I thought I deserved. All the time I wasted that could have been spent with family and friends who have now passed away. I stayed away from them because they knew me when I had a daughter. All the joys I could have had sooner if I would have been on God's time schedule. His dreams for me in 1986 were then and are always so much greater than my own limited ability to think and dream.

But I had sentenced myself to a life of seclusion, emptiness, and pain from 1984 to about 1991. I walked away from every friend but Sheila and Mary Lou who knew me before the accident. I kept myself from all of those people who cared for me because of the guilt I felt for driving the car Michelle died in. I could not stand to see the looks in everyone's eyes and to believe they, too, thought me guilty.

Only If

On that Saturday night, I realized I had been wrong all these years. I had kept myself from feeling the love, support and friendship that would have been there if I would have allowed myself the grace to receive it. If I had only had the courage to ask for it, but I feared their rejection.

All the years of pain might have ended so much sooner if I had allowed myself to share my pain so they could have shared theirs as well. Now I think that perhaps the look in everyone's eyes had been their pain, their loss and their compassion they needed to share with me. Their love they needed to express to me. I took it as their blame to feed the guilt I was feeling and my life I thought I deserved.

The cards that were meant to comfort me seventeen years ago did that at last and so much more. I carefully put each card in its envelope, lovingly bundled them up and placed them in the suitcase MJ would bring to me on her visit to Maui. That night I had that warm and fuzzy feeling Joyce tried to explain to me one day, but had no memory of ever experiencing.

I released the regrets for what might have been or never was, since they are now part of my past. A past I cannot change today no matter what actions I take. I can only change how I let the choices and regrets of the past affect me today. I cannot let the past spoil my today and cast a shadow on all my tomorrows.

That Saturday night I felt as though I was sleeping with angels surrounding my bed. I am sure the angels have always been there these seventeen years, but that night I allowed myself to feel their unconditional love. I allowed myself to be comforted. I allowed myself to become part of the vast scheme of things. I slept the sleep of an innocent child at long last.

Only If

September 11, 2001

Every morning when I awake, I turn on *Good Morning America*. I have been getting my daily news fix and views of the world from GMA since Joan London had her first child. Charlie Gibson and Diane Sawyer were there on duty on September 11, 2001. I was sitting on the edge of the bed as the first plane hit the Twin Towers of the World Trade Center. I was still there as the second plane hit. I made a cup of coffee and watched transfixed at the words and pictures evolved.

I had to do something. There was no furniture left in my home and nothing to clean since the estate sale was held nearly a month ago. The remnants of my life were now in piles and rows in the garage. I got dressed and moved the last of the televisions into the garage, filled my thermos and watched television as I sorted through the last of my personal items.

I prepared the box for the non-profit agency as the first tower fell and I wept. I was sorting the stuff for the Salvation Army as the second tower fell and sat down struck with grief. One after another, the buildings fell as I sorted through the last vestiges of my life.

My friend, Joyce, was teaching in England. We kept in touch since 1997 via emails. It is hard to recreate my feelings of that day and the days to follow. I have chosen to copy the two letters I wrote her concerning the events of those days. My letters are in answer to the letters she wrote to me. I hope you can read between the lines and follow my train of thought. I could not respond to her emails the first two days. I was in shock, as I am sure many of us were. These are answers to her questions and concern – the concerns of an American living and teaching in England on September 11, 2001.

Subject: I can now speak.
Date: Thursday, September 13, 2001 10:22 PM

I have no doubt, whatsoever, that we will heal. Not only heal, as a nation, but as in the past, we will survive, conquer, and lead the free world. We will wipe our tears, put tissues in our pocket, put on our gloves, put our collective shoulders to the wheel, and grow and live and lead.

We will open our hearts and our pocketbooks. We are a nation of patriotic people. Patriotic in the way a large portion of our free world is. Here are some stories I have heard about the last few days that may or may not have reached your airwaves or newspapers in England. Some give me hope and renew my spirit and keep glowing my burning heart of patriotism. Some fill me with pain, but I too will heal. I have before and I will again:

> When the crew of workers reached the center of the carnage, they placed a recently cut pine tree on top the highest point of the rubble. Many of the first groups of volunteers were construction people from New York City and surrounding areas. They thought that since they constructed these buildings, they might be able to be of some help. In the construction trade when you reach the highest point of your construction, out of reverence to our natural resources you are using, they place a recently cut tree as a symbol

of respect. It was placed on top of the approximate six floors of the rubble of the 110-story tower.

> The people of New York City, not being able to dig or physically help, have formed a human chain extending for blocks and blocks, on the route the rescue workers take, the ambulances travel, the dump trucks lumber along, the doctors and nurses ride. They cheer and clap and hold signs of "Thank you" and "We love you." Those leaving the carnage cry. Those entering are motivated to do even more.

> Rescue workers, when told to leave after a 12 hours shift, weep from the sights they have seen. Though exhausted, they want to stay and keep digging. They leave only when they realize they are not capable of giving their best under their present condition.

> There has been a call for blood. So many people have offered nationwide, the Red Cross had to make appointments into the next weeks to take the blood that has been offered.

> The fancy eating places of New York City – ones you and I can hardly afford to sniff, let alone eat at – are making food for the rescue workers, displaced persons, those waiting for words, anyone who has a need.

> One restaurant near the presently called "dead zone," closed their doors to food to provide a place for people to sleep.

> People were standing in long lines trying to use the few pay phones still working to let their loved ones know they were alright. Those who passed by, seeing the long wait, offered cell phones to call anywhere the cell phone range would be able to reach.

> Taxicabs tore their back seats out so bodies could be taken from the scene. Flatbed trucks arrived later to take over this task. No bodies were recovered. Each day the expected death toll goes up by a few hundred – these

Only If

are the ones we only know are missing – 4,700 today. I expected 30,000. Now 20,000 body bags are available in New York. Less than 200 bodies have been recovered so far. Some bodies have been discovered, but you cannot get to them due to continued fires, tightly knit debris, and tons upon tons of rubble.

> We heard stories Tuesday night of someone with a cell phone saying they were trapped and when and please come to get me. The phone calls stopped early Wednesday morning.

> Doctors and nurses, called to all the hospitals to handle the injured on Tuesday, today went home for lack of work. This is not good news. No work means no one to save.

> USS Comfort, a hospital ship, arrived in NY harbor yesterday to help handle the injured. So far, there is no need.

> We were all so thrilled today to find out seven men had been rescued. The radio said two men we caught under a wall collapse today, and while digging them out, they found five firefighters in an SUV from Tuesday. This went over the airwaves and so much hope came forth. When I got home I searched CNN and MSNBC for the story.

> Two men were buried under a small collapse today. One firefighter heard the noise and arrived on the scene when the firefighters had gone down to help and pulled out the two. The overwrought firefighter misunderstood the events and was so excited that seven of the 202 missing firefighters and 82 missing officers had been found! The news reporter did not check it out and broadcasted a false story. Our hope cascaded again. Is there any hope with the fires and rubble?

> Today President Bush had a televised phone conference with the Governor of New York, George Pataki and Mayor of New York City, Rudy

Only If

Giuliani. They discussed via the television and radio his plan to go to New York tomorrow and thank the workers and go to St. Patrick's Cathedral to lead a National Day of Prayer. After the phone call, the President took questions from the reporters present. During his response to some of the questions, you could see his pain, quivering mouth edges and his eyes filled with tears. He said something to the effect that he was a loving man, but was resolute in his commitment to bring these terrorists to justice and save the whole world and the USA from terrorists.

> It is heartwarming to see the Democrats and Republicans band together for the good of the nation. I hope they will remember this solidarity and "good of the nation" when things get back to normal–whatever and whenever that may be. This IS the way our politicians should act all the time. They are our representatives and are supposed to work for our good and not the photo ops and opportunities in general.

> I do not like the photo opportunities some of the politicians are taking. I know NY needs to be visible and so does the president, but men from other states should stay away from the microphones.

> Today, at my gas station, there was a shoebox decorated in red, white, and blue with the message,, "For your dimes and dollars for the people of New York and Washington D.C."

> On Wednesday, one local radio announcer went to several craft stores in town and purchased all the red, white and blue ribbon. The radio station employees made bows and the announcer (without a microphone or publicity) went to downtown Green Bay to hand out the bows for people to wear to support the people of New York and show our patriotism. When our mayor heard of this, his staff went to Appleton to purchase more ribbon and is taking up this practice today and tomorrow.

Only If

> Tuesday and Wednesday EVERY church in Green Bay held masses, services or prayer vigils. The place and time of services were run on local television station under the national programs on television.

> The flight data recorder has been discovered from the Pennsylvania plane crash. Not the voice recorder, but data recorder. That is amazing considering the thirty-foot-deep trench and ashes at the crash site.

> Fire broke out again tonight at the Pentagon.

> Today we heard there were four people who called from the Pennsylvania airplane. All told of the hijacking. We were told the people on this plane knew what had happened to the other three planes. We were told that two callers said there were a group of patriotic men on the plane who were going to overtake the hijackers and make sure this plane did not hit the White House or any other place. We are hopeful they crashed the plane to sacrifice their lives to save so many unknown numbers more. Notice I said sacrifice and not suicide.

> Today a company in Minnesota is making, unasked and free of charge, leather footies for dogs. There are many glass slivers in the rubble and the rescue dogs' feet are being cut and injured. The need for the cadaver hunting dogs will be even greater in the following days. These footies will protect the dogs' paws.

> Tony Blair's support has been heard and greatly appreciated all week long.

> Tonight on CNN I saw an international response for the first time. I had watched BBC on Tuesday and Wednesday night, but saw only the British reporters retelling CNN news. But tonight I was very touched by the response from England. I saw the flowers being placed in memory of the lives lost. I saw the signs of support from the people, Margaret Thatcher

signing a condolence card. I heard the Changing of the Guard playing our "Star Spangled Banner." I get goose pimples as I think of it even now.

> Mike takes many international customer service calls. He is keeping a log of comments of support from the clients from other countries. They are in pain, as are we, and want to express it to someone in the USA, and Mike is right here in Wisconsin taking international calls. They express their sadness, outrage, pain, prayer, hope for discovery.

We are:
One Nation - One Free World - Under God. But,
Our God Is A God Of Love And Not Vengeance.
Our God Is A God Of Peace And Not Retribution.
Our God Is A God Of Sacrifice Not Suicide.
Our God Is A God Of Prosperity And Not Persecution.

Yes, we will heal. We will survive. We will prevail. We will lead. We will love.

Please thank your friends and fellow teachers for the support they have shown. It means much to me, to all of us. I can now speak. I will heal. I will lead. I will follow. I will prevail.

Love, Linda

Only If

Subject: My thoughts on "War"
Date: Thursday, September 27, 2001 8:02 PM

Dear Joyce:

I must apologize to you for not reading your letter of September 21 in which you had a subject of war. I am so sorry I was too busy to read it any sooner than today. I went to Sheila's Friday and have been running since I returned home late Sunday. It is 7 p.m. and your letter to me and mine to you was the first on my list for this evening.

I am sorry the events in New York had such a negative effect on you, Joyce. It must be strange to be in a foreign country, from a country of peace, as is the USA, and have England sort of questioning the viability of you staying in their country. Rather strange indeed, when England has been fighting a religious war for how many years now? But, you must admit, you would be so much safer and it would be easier to protect if you were here. Our nation is safer today than it was pre-911. Coming home is coming home. A job is irrelevant if you feel unsafe or unwelcome in a foreign land. Only you can decide.

I can well remember in the 1950s when everyone was building bomb shelters to protect their families from the nuclear attack from Russia. I remember listening to a conversation between my parents about how we had a good stash of canned goods in the basement. We "would be all right." And that has been my attitude about events such as this – we will be all right.

I can remember in summer 1963, when I had graduated from high school and was living in my first apartment. I called my Aunt Dettie in Middleton asking if the world was coming to an end. A group of East Indian religious zealots were conducting a physical prayer circle because the planets were going to be in a specific alignment and this denoted the end of the world. My Aunt Dettie soothed me.

I feel we have always been on the brink of war since we dropped the A-bomb on Japan and devastated so many lives and a country. We helped to rebuild the country and they came to attack us (at least it is my thought) in our economy. Doing things better, faster, and cheaper than we can, and our Americans buying Japanese products and helping their economy and weakening ours.

At one point, during the Cuban Missile Crisis, we were to be about five seconds to destruction of the world for most of the time. I understand that clock moved backward a few seconds when the Cold War with Russia ended. I have often wondered how that clock was affected with events like the Gulf War, Granada, Afghanistan's invasion from Russians and our support of them, the capture and imprisonment of our men in Iran, Saddam Hussein, Muammar Gaddafi …

The list can, and does, go on and on and on endlessly. As an individual I cannot effect a change on the activities of our nation to, for, or against another. They do their thing physically and our nation responds. If I do not like what they do, the people in charge of our country, I can cast a vote. That is usually not immediately effective either. Names and commitments change, but fear and evil does exist in the world. Always has and always will.

However, there is something I can do and I do try to do it to the best of my ability. I admit I was numb at the onslaught of September 11th. I sort of shut myself off so I did not feel, but gathered the information from four or five television stations, radio programs, papers, and listened to friends and public officials. I, too, am a baby boomer. I heard the stories of WWII from elderly uncles. Bob Wells periodically shared watered-down stories of Korea to spare my soul pain. I remember the uproar on Vietnam. I did live through that, but I was a married woman at the time and less affected than others of my age.

Yes, this was a horrific act that was committed to the people in New York and Washington, D.C. and in that field in Pennsylvania. Their loved ones experienced the loss, they suffered, they grieve, and their lives will be so different than any of them dreamed of when they went to bed Monday night on September 10th. Lives, futures and dreams were lost by those people living and dying there.

The nature of the world I now live in has undergone a change as well, and so have I. I am a little more mindful of my surroundings, but will not be reclusive and I will not cower. I am a little more reflective and a lot more thankful for what I have. A lot more prayerful and now include the world rather than just those who are emotionally close. At a distance from me, my motherhood and sisterhood is now the world.

The most effective change I can have on the world at large, whether on this issue or any issue, is to have an effect on those in my personal circle. I will still continue to practice unconditional love, compassion, empathy, understanding, tolerance, and acceptance. And continue to live my life in a manner I believe to be honorable and one worth emulating if someone would choose to do so.

I must believe what I am saying because, for a fleeting moment, I thought about not moving to Hawaii. Then I remembered that this is my time and someone in the Middle East will not keep me down. All the efforts of the Universe have come together for me at this time in my life. Physical work by me, thanksgiving from me, blind trust and acceptance of His will in the matter of my move. My God is in control of my Universe and all will be well with me. I am not fearful here or will I be fearful on Maui. I am safe–all will be well.

As for the world at large, many prayers are needed from us as individuals. It is the most effective thing we can do outside of projecting positive characteristics and attributes to others we come in contact with on a day-to-day basis. Listen, understand, comfort if we can, but project confidence in the USA and in our president that he is capable of taking care of us as a people so much better than Clinton ever would have. Thank God, Bush is President at this time in our history. He is an honorable man. He is a family man. He is thinking and feeling man. He is a common man called to greatness. He will lead this nation, if not the world to a resolution of this matter.

We will be at war. We are at war. We have been at war for many years now. This war will be different. We saw in the Gulf War that it was conducted, for the most part, from thousands of feet in the air and sort of a "video game" war with technology being the strength, our lifeblood, and not the blood of our brave men and women. Yes, blood will be spilled. It will be awful at times. But the world cannot let the butchering of humanity on September 11th ever happen again. And, it must be stopped at all possible speed. It does not have to happen tomorrow or the day after. It is very important we are 100 percent correct and just as effective when the peacemakers of the world take out the faction that perpetrated this on the free world and Christian world at large.

So, I will do the best I can to keep things under control and on the right path on my home front. That is the only front I can be effective in. I will pray for peace and correctiveness and thoroughness. I will not cower. I will not be depressed. I will not defeat myself and I will not let them defeat me.

Thanks for pulling this out of me. I have never verbalized this before, much less formulated the thoughts in any manner. I just answer as you ask. You do bring things out in me for better or for worse. I do so love the opportunity to pull together my beliefs and values when they are asked of me.

I want to extend my love and peace to you, dear friend. Consider my arms around you and hugging you and telling you that "you will heal, but it will take time." Did I ever tell you this phrase was spoken to me in my mind's eye?

It happened in 1986 as I sat on the rock at the base of the Seven Sacred Pools on Maui. It was my first trip to Maui. The ocean was a green-blue I have never seen before or since. The salty spray of the ocean was gently caressing my face. I could taste the salt on my lips. The creamy yellow sea foam from the waves crashing at the base of my rock was attaching itself to various parts of my body.

I found myself looking down at me on that rock. I looked up the path the river followed from the top of the volcano to the base of the ocean at my feet. I saw twenty-one Sacred Pools and not seven. Then I heard "you will heal, but it will take time. You will heal, but it will take time." At that moment in my life I knew from the depths of my soul and felt I was loved. I knew I would be all right. He told me so. That moment of peace, tranquility, love, acceptance, and happiness has been a focal point and has pulled me and carried me through many events in my life since 1986. It has been my center. It is a moment I have lusted after. It is a life I have now achieved.

Only If

    I hope you can find something to sustain you. For you to find a focus, a center. I have had my experience that means so much to me. I can do no more for you than to pray, accept you, and to continue to be your dear Friend as you are mine.

Love, Linda

Only If

Only If

Falling Into Place

Fall hit Wisconsin at last, and I made my very last trip to a client's home nearly two hours away. Though the drive is long, I always enjoyed the journey. I make good time on a four-lane highway for half of the trip, then a westward running two-lane state road. I pass through a few small towns, but most of the last half of my trip is through softly curving roads and gently rolling hills. Pure farmland at its finest.

Now with shorter days and colder nights, the Canadian geese were making their first feeble attempts to get into a streamline V formation. It was reminiscent of what I imagine army boot camp and the first day a new recruit would try to fit in to the marching pattern. It made me chuckle to see the birds trying to make a simple formation.

Fields once green with sweet corn and golden tassels waving in the breezes were now nothing but short and silver stubs after having their crop cut to the ground. I passed through the town of Pickett on my way. There is a canning factory there. Huge semis were dropping off sweet corn at one end of the plant. Bulldozers put the corn on conveyer belts to go into the factory for processing. At the other end of the plant, the spent husks and ground cobs were exiting. There was a smaller dozer on the pile with a large, flat roof to protect the driver. A football field-sized pile was 12 to 15 feet tall, and they were moving the new layer out to flatten the pile.

Only If

Further down Highway 44, the once-pale tan oat fields were now golden with straw shafts left after harvesting. Flocks of all types of birds hovered over and landed on the newly harvested fields for their share of the fallen oat and wheat grains. Fields of soybeans were a deep golden and brown, now ready for one of my clients in Omro to harvest.

Yes, the fields, animals, and now the people knew fall was approaching. The temperature gets only into the upper 60s, if we're lucky. The cooler nights and shorter days start the trees to change colors and display their beauty to me one last time. The drive along the Fox River to Green Bay was breathtaking, as the placid river reflected the orange, red, gold, and sporadic green leaves. Then there was the rain every few days, as is the custom of fall. The grass in my yard was a lush green and my flowers never looked better. They were all bidding me a fond, luscious and beautiful farewell.

I made one last trip to Wausau to see my friend Sheila and her boys. How does one say goodbye yet again to a friend of twenty-four years? We have maintained this friendship over the years and have lived in the same community for only three of those years. It won't cost any more to call from Hawaii than it does from Wrightstown, thanks to phone cards. Our friendship will not suffer; just the one-to-one personal visits will. As I left Sheila's home for the last time, my heart was heavy with the last goodbye and filled with the expectation of what my new home would bring.

The drive home from Wausau was full of rain, but the trees really looked beautiful halfway between Wausau and Green Bay. Fall comes earlier to the Central Wisconsin area around Highway 45 and Wittenberg. The trees were about 75 percent turned. The reds and golds and oranges almost sparkled in the lightly falling rain. Mother Nature was dressed in her finest for me to see one last time.

One of the people who toured my home at the estate sale made an offer on my home. And I accepted. It was contingent on the FHA inspection. All I needed to do was put in a GFI outlet where the washer and dryer are, and put a metal plate over the outlet where the spa was wired in 1987. So I have passed all the tests. The original offer on my home wanted $1,000 for repairs! Only $32 in repairs were needed. It does not cost to maintain your home–it only pays.

I got a little excited at the accepted offer. Guess I was talking a mile a minute as I told MJ the good news about the inspection and it meant the deal would go through. I could feel my pulse racing and excitement rising, but managed to get control myself. I did not want to get too involved in emotions until I was on the way to my bank with the signed check. Old adages like "don't count your chickens before they hatch" and "pride goeth before the fall" kept dancing in my mind. Could this all really be true after the months and months of physical labor? After all the sorting, giving away, and selling my personal possessions after all the years of having the dream, could this really be coming true?

Then the next day dawned to reveal yet another beautiful Indian summer day. I got just what I asked for by spending fall in Wisconsin. The day temperatures made it to the 70s those last few days. The weather was perfect. The trees and changing colors were magnificent and I took photos to help me preserve my memories of fall. All the little details of my life and my move were falling into place. I got a little sunburn mowing the yard for the last time. I did the weed eater thing for the last time, I hope, I hope, I hope! The riding mower would be going to Jody and Glenn soon.

Only If

I vacuumed the garage out one last time and checked the piles going to charity. They go in two days.

There was a pile for Michael that he and his two friends would pick up my last weekend in my home.

I called my car movers. It will take one month to ship my car if they pick it up at my door. I am going that route, but not until I have my closing check.

Sheila's daughter, Michelle, came from Oshkosh to get the last of the stuff she purchased.

Pam will come in two weeks to get the bed, rocker and file cabinet, and then I will go to a hotel unless I want to sleep on an air mattress.

My contact in Hawaii has been invaluable to me. Guiding me to places to rent and then checking them out for me. Thanks to his efforts, I now have a room in Makawao to rent for a month while I look for a home to rent.

It is difficult to recall all that I did those last weeks in my home. Little tasks here and there, washing this, repacking that. I took in a few pairs of pants and hemmed several others, decided not to bring my sewing machine. Time for a new one! Isn't it strange how losing weight makes pants longer? There are three pairs of new summer weight pants to hem, but that will have to be done in Hawaii where I will need them. Wonder if they wear white all year round?

I washed out the last two cupboards that the last little bit of food was stored in, and then hit all the outside of the cupboards again with a cleaner. Skipped the tops of the cupboards, thank you. Been there, done that. I did a final cleaning of the oven as well.

I had five opened boxes in the otherwise-empty second bedroom. I pick up something here and deposit it there. I packed and unpacked one box three times. Finally I completed the inventory of the box, gave it an alphabetic letter "C," sealed it, and called it done. Three down and two to go!

I am glad I made the decision to pack my bedroom ensemble. Since I vacillated on the decision so much, MJ said to pack it. It is light and will cost less to ship than some of the stuff I have in suitcases. I washed the two sets of sheets I kept and the comforter, and packed them away. Interspersed with all the soft bedding material are the really special things I cannot part with.

I have all the sunset pictures out of the frames, Tupperware containers have the family photos in them and they are nestled between the sheets. I kept the plaster cast hands from the kids as they entered first grade. I have the photo and frame of the kids taken the Christmas before Michelle died, and the cross from Michelle's casket. Some things you just keep, no matter what.

Mike will transport the books, audios and videotapes I have chosen to take with me. MJ will take a suitcase, too. She will bring the mementoes of Michelle with her and my artificial flowers from my bedroom arrangements. Next weekend I will wash and pack the drapes, valance and sheers, and then that will fill my "B" box.

There are just a few last things to clear up for clients. I need to edit and print out three sets of computer procedure finger strokes for three people I have been training. Life does go on, no matter how tired one is.

By October 1st there were just fifteen days to closing! I babbled on and on like a blithering idiot those days. My adrenaline was pretty much out of control. The excitement was wearing me down. Stress from joy is almost as debilitating as it is from sorrow and depression. I prefer joy though. One by one I crossed off the jobs to be done. Unfortunately, there always seems to be one more thing I added to the list, but not the ten or fifteen more I added when I started this project in March. My list did get smaller each day!

My friend, Wendy, made a generous offer for me to stay with her from October 14 to my departure date. Departure will not be definite until I close. My last day of client commitment was October 26. Wendy says she loves to hear me speak. Apparently, I am even more animated than usual and was slightly giddy those days. ("Oh, grow up, Linda!")

I felt like Alastair Sims in *A Christmas Carol*, playing Ebenezer Scrooge. I well remember the morning after the three spirits visited him. He was clicking his heels and jumping for joy at the prospects of life. In his office he starts to laugh and then he raps the desk and says, "I am so happy I cannot stand it!" Well, that was me those last few days in my home.

The time arrived for me to make contact with my friends and family. Following is the letter I sent out over the internet. I am so glad I kept these letters and a journal. They have been invaluable to me in the creation of this book:

October 4, 2001

Dear Friends and Family:

It's me again. Bet you never thought you would hear from me so soon. Time moves at its own pace. We can either go along for the ride or fight a never-ending battle of going against the tide and flow of life. I am along for the ride, and what a ride it has been, is, and will continue to be for me.

Had a local couple look at my home three times last week. Today at 10:30, I got a call from my agent. The third counteroffer has been accepted. The closing will be October 15 - so I won't need to spend too much money on hotels before I fly off to Maui! I will not believe it until I am on the way to the bank with the check, but it looks really good. I passed the inspection from FHA and the bank, so it is a go.

Everything has fallen in place so far, so I know this will as well. This cannot be as physically demanding as I have gone through the first 90 days to get my home ready to sell! I have several leads already on possible living arrangements once I hit Maui, and I will follow up on them as the time draws near. When the closing is done, I will have my car shipped to Maui and rent a car here for a week or two.

It amazes me how things fall into place when I sit back and let God handle it all. All I have to do is my part, to be prepared, to respond to things that need to be done,–and to work my butt off! My rewards are many faceted. I am at peace and very calm with the confidence that this move is ordained and meant to be and will be relatively effortless.

I have been here this summer to see my annual bedding plants in full bloom. The red weigila bush was ablaze with its red trumpet flowers that will continue to bloom into early October. The orange tiger lilies, acquired from a roadside "reallocation of natural resources" with a neighbor Judy, were brilliant this summer with flower heads nearly six feet in the air just outside my picture window. They are reflected in my living room in the artificial floral arrangements I had made and are now gracing the living room of a 70-year-old neighbor.

The white Shasta daisies were especially large this year and have tripled in plant width the past two years. The bright yellow daylilies opened on time just behind the Shastas and spilled their heady fragrances in my bedroom window for well over a month this summer.

Only If

The nearby ruby red daylilies have faded now, but covered a three-square-foot area of the flowerbed. The ground cover I planted last fall and this spring have all taken hold and are getting taller and sending out long tendrils to cover the mulch eventually. The flowerbeds have never looked better. It is the way I have always wanted it to look – and just in the nick of time!

I have taken a photo or two throughout the summer and have forgotten all the backbreaking effort I put into these flowerbeds the past fourteen years. Joyce and many of you have heard my tales of quack grass and dandelions all these years. Now I will never have to battle with those two demons again!
Now I know a young family will have a lovely new and energy efficient home to move into and continue their life together. The sound of children will bounce off the walls instead of Home and Garden TV. The Cartoon Network will replace Oprah, The Discovery Channel, A&E and TLC. The backyard is large and will give ample room to add on and still have a great play yard and a vegetable garden if they want. I could not have asked for anything more than that. I am so pleased. Oh, did I tell you? My home was sold to someone who toured the home at the estate sale! Sheila's signs and the guided tours did the trick.

On warm summer nights, I will miss the sounds of the church bell in my backyard at 9 p.m., 10 p.m. 11 p.m., and midnight–if I managed to stay awake that long. I will miss the call of the 11 p.m. train traveling through town. Both of these brought forth the memories of youthful summer nights in Goodman. I will miss the purple finches eating my orange slices and keeping my company for so many spring, summer and fall mornings. The robins' and mourning doves' calls will be no more.

Only If

I will miss listening to the distant rumble of an approaching thunderstorm and then the sounds of the rain on my garage roof. I will miss the smell of the approaching rain and the sweetness of the earth after it passes. I will miss the sun rising in my front window and making my living room orange as the morning lights filter through those tangerine curtains.

I will miss the gathering of the Hat Ladies and our nights by my waterfall, the tiki lamps, the salmon on the grill, the margaritas, tortilla chips and dip, and tons of laughter and moments of magic we shared together. I will miss my aunt and cousins spending a few nights with me, our bingo games and one-armed bandit experiences. My heart and memories are filled to overflowing. One can never have too many memories or too much love to carry in their soul.

For all I am leaving behind in Wisconsin, I will be rewarded with endless summer nights in Hawaii. There will be new birds and flowers to learn about and enjoy with my morning and evening coffee. Perhaps there will be fresh fruits right in my own backyard. However, my gardening experience will be limited to container gardening and someone to do the lawn work, or I won't rent it!

The ever-present trade winds will fill my home and mind with scents of the South Sea Islands. The brisk winds will make the days cooler and refreshing instead of the cold and bitter Wisconsin winters that are five months long. If I can afford it, I will have a sunrise or sunset each day to fill my home with the real thing instead of photos and pictures on the walls–but the photos are coming with me, too, by the way.

I will make trips to the ocean to feel the power and watch the majesty of the waves. The feel and taste of the salt spray will tingle my face. Perhaps,

Only If

if I look carefully, I will see the spirit of Gardner McKay at the helm of his sailing schooner. I hope so, for he started the dream in 1959.

I am moving to the island God created just for me, or anyone who has the desire, drive, and perhaps a little bit of courage. To those I love, I ask that you do go after your dream and live in your own personal paradise - wherever or whatever it may be. Think of me as you dream. And remember, your dreams are your realities that are yet to be, only if you have the dream and do the work to make it happen. If I can make my dream come true at this age, it cannot be as difficult for you.

Will I see you there in my paradise? If not, you will be in my thoughts as I travel the island. I will relish the memories we have shared together as I create new ones on Hawaii. And, I will see you on the internet.

Aloha to all.
Much love, Linda

Only If

Five Days To Closing

If my Janet Court neighborhood had any doubts I was moving, they knew it this day. On the night before my last trash day, I hired a neighborhood teenager who took all of my leftovers to the roadside. We hauled it to the curb in a blowing rain. Fortunately, it was a warm and balmy night, more like a spring evening than October 11th. It was a deal for me for $20. So the last remnant of my home in Wrightstown and my life in Wisconsin ended up at roadside, ready for the dump.

Now the bed, television and a suitcase were all that remained in my bedroom. The desk was sold to a neighbor to be disassembled and taken when I leave my home on the 14th. A client took my leather chair earlier that day. The file cabinet, bed, ladder and television was to go to Pam that Saturday. No food or dishes or glasses or pots or pans remained in my home. However, I did have the essential coffee, a pot and two coffee cups–ever hopeful for company.

My office had my computer still ready to do my bidding. I continued to scan papers into my computer and save on discs. I had a banker's box of papers to bring to Hawaii, but was having a hard time justifying the price to ship it. Sheila took my tax papers from 1995 to date. She will bring them to Hawaii if and when she comes. Each year she will toss the oldest dates. I made a copy of the 1040s for the past three years to take to Hawaii in case I need them.

MJ, Wendy and Sheila said they had never heard me talk so fast in all the years they have known me. I was not the calm, cool and collected person they have known. I was on a high that could not be downed! I felt like a bottle of sparkling champagne and I was overflowing with every happy emotion known to man and womankind. This effervescence sapped my energy as badly as depression did for most of my life, but I rebounded quickly and found even more energy than before.

I will get it all done. There is plenty of time. I have gotten more accomplished than I have left to do. I was thinking of hemming pants on the plane, but wondered if I can do them if I don't have a scissors, since they are banned now? Screw the plane! I want to read, not mend! At this rate, I won't even need a plane to get there, I will fly solo! I am a blissfully happy, content and successful person who is moving to Hawaii to make a dream come true. I am not someone who is chucking it all to move to Hawaii and hopes to become blissfully happy, content and become a success. I am a success.

October 13, 2001

Dear Hat Ladies,

It is 4:30 p.m. and I am about to go to Green Bay and sleep at Wendy's home. My home is empty except for the office stuff I am packing up. I have just finished cleaning the bathroom and kitchen for the last time, hopefully. I plan to make a quick stop at Judy's and then to Green Bay. I will return Sunday and do some backing up and tearing down the computer while I watch my last Packer game.

Only If

I cannot believe my great good fortune in the consummation of all my efforts and embarking on this adventure to Hawaii. All of you have been so supportive. I know, at times, this all sounded rather wild, even to me and I conceived the idea. However, as the day draws closer, I realize this is the culmination of so many hours of wishing and dreaming. And forty years of thinking how cool it would be to live on a tropical island in the South Seas – if only. Now I realize a dream happens – only if.

Many a sunny morning were spent in the big chair in the living room, often snuggled into a mohair blanket or a handmade coral afghan, watching the rising sun fill my living room with the warmth of the new day. Many a cold winter's nights were made warmer by the thoughts of swaying palm trees and large ocean waves pounding the sandy beaches. I have dreamed of cloud shrouded volcano peeks and sweeping sunrises and sunsets flickering on the endless white-capped seas.

I can see myself stepping out on a lanai with a cup of coffee and watching the sunrise as the morning breezes blow my brightly colored caftan! These two caftans have been to Hawaii three times and they are coming for one more trip. I got these two caftans back in 1986 for my first trip to Maui. They came along in 1991 to Kauai with my Aunt Sadie and in 2000 to Oahu and Maui with Michael. They are a little worn and mended a time or two, but still, they deserve a trip to Maui, one last time. As do I.

Thank you for being there for me as I worked through the past few months. Forgive me for not sharing my dream with you sooner than I did. I needed it to be my little secret for some of the time in case my initial fact-finding and spurt of jobs to be done became more powerful than my dream to move to Maui.

Only If

This is the last letter from Wrightstown. Will be on line shortly at Wendy's.

Night,
Linda

I always thought that offices were the junk collector of the world. I now know that my office was the Mecca for collection. I owe Wendy big time for the bags and boxes of stuff I had to toss into her Dumpster after my weekend of sorting. I got back to my home office at 9:10 a.m. that Sunday morning, and was not ready to tear apart the computer until 3:30 p.m. I managed to fill banker's boxes of items yet to be winnowed out, or pay the shipping fee to Hawaii at $1.13 per pound.

I had two weeks left to do that. I would fly out on October 30th. The 30th! Oh my God, My God!!! Here I go again!

The Fox River is one of only a few rivers in the USA that flows to the north, and it runs through the middle of Wrightstown. That last night the Fox was very still. The bright red, orange and yellow autumn-colored trees and the colors of the setting sun reflected on the river as if it were a mirror. The sun was setting as I drove to the highway for the last time.

It is strange, but this was one of the few times I was able to see the sun set on the western horizon. The church and stand of trees in my neighbor's back yard had always blocked my views of sunsets and I only saw the afterglows these past fourteen years. But oh, those sunrises I was treated to! So now the die had been cast, and I needed to say goodbye to Wrightstown.

Only If

The night before the closing was my second night at Wendy's, and I got really excited. This is going to happen after all, isn't it? I had no problems sleeping after the long and taxing day. However, at 7:00 that morning, I woke up startled from a dream, thinking I still had five rooms of ornate, dark brown furniture to unload to some unsuspecting Brazilian, for that was the taste of the furniture filling my home in my dream. Heck, it was a nightmare!

Then I realized I only had a few boxes left in this bedroom to complete and dozed on and off, still trying to find someone to take this furniture off my hands so I could move to Hawaii. Wow, I must have had some unresolved stress to get off my shoulders. I needed to realize that most of my work was done.

October 16, 2001

The closing went without a hitch. The new owner and her agent had a walk-though of my home in the morning before closing. She found the bottle of Asti and two champagne glasses I left on the counter with the book of equipment papers. They checked out the storm windows that were now installed after the air conditioners were removed. They checked out the GFI and plate added in the basement – my only two repairs needed.

I was calm, cool and collected at the table as I signed all those forms. It was easy to sign away my property. My "home" would travel within me to Hawaii. We chatted back and forth as the papers moved around the huge table. And then it was done.

The ride home after the closing was a strange one indeed. I made it out of the office fine and managed to find my way from downtown Appleton to

Only If

Highway 41. Once I was on the highway, I started to cry and did so for most of the twenty-five miles to Green Bay.

These were tears of joy and of pride. Tears of the realization that I was actually going to move to Maui! Tears of appreciation for what I have been given in my life. It was all so unbelievable. I pulled out my rosary as I drove past the Wrightstown turn off and said another one of my Rosary of Thankfulness for all blessing I have been given.

It was easy to be more relaxed with the closing completed. I could now have dinner out with friends, one-on-one every couple days, and go through the final appointments with all my clients and last-minute training of my replacements. I was greeted with well wishes, hugs, and gifts. What was not to be relaxed about?

Karen and her staff at Hilly Haven Golf Course showered me with gifts. Knowing I like to write, I got a special pen to write the staff and to use for my stories. There was a card signed by all that held two dinner theatre tickets for the coming weekend.

And Karen, the ever-wonderful, observant and kind person she is, arranged for a foot massage. She noticed the pain I was experiencing as the closing came closer and closer. It was particularly bad after closing my home over the weekend. So on my second visit to her office that week, she informed me that I had an appointment at 1 o'clock with a foot massage therapist. I hobbled into that office and pranced out.

I was so relaxed that I totally wasted the rest of the day at the golf course office, fighting to not slip off the leather office chair. To end my day, she had one of the guys take me on a tour of the beautifully manicured golf course. I had my first experience in a golf cart traversing over bridges, around corners and thorough the giant and ever-colorful oak, maple, and birch trees in their autumn splendor and aromas.

I was in a very positive state of being, and have been so for several years now. It is the way I choose to live my life. I do the things I can and have learned to accept when things come up that I cannot change. I will continue my travel through life at my own speed, taking responsibility for my actions and my life and allowing others the same opportunity to learn and grow.

I have learned that if I wanted to change my life, I had to change my thinking. I had to change the way I acted, reacted and responded. I learned to listen twice as much as I talked. I learned to hear with my heart. I learned to give advice when asked and say it in a nurturing way. This is a life of learning, and as long as I have breath, it is never, ever too late to learn, to change, to grow, to evolve, and to love.

I choose to live life as I plan and not be influenced by lazy or ineffective people. I will not allow myself to be swayed by the demands and actions of religious zealots in the Middle East. This is my time in life. It is time for me to do as I will. As I choose. As I desire. I am secure in my values. I know I have honorable intentions and am confident of my skills.

Thank you, God, for the gifts and blessing you have given me.

Only If

Only If

The Sendoff

The Hat Ladies had a little sendoff for me. We were quite an attention-gathering group. Not by our noise, but by our appearance. We had only set a tropical theme–we are a theme-based group. There were no calls back and forth to check out what each other was wearing. But we all appeared in brightly colored clothing, and each one of us had flowers in our hair! Some wore a fresh lei, some used artificial flowers. I wore a floor-length black dress that has a printed lavender-shaded, sleeveless jacket over the top. I went to Parmentier's Floral and had a fresh arrangement for my right ear.

Everyone looked so great! We had so much fun. Two of the ladies gave me disposable cameras for pictures of Hawaii. Pam gave me two cameras so we could use one that night and the other for my first days on Hawaii.

Countless people came up to us and asked what the occasion was. Some took photos for us. Some took photos with us. It was Sweetest Day, and the place was full of couples. There we were, all these forty-five and older Hat Ladies dressed all in reds, purples, lime greens, yellows, and hot pinks, and most everyone else was in basic black or dull fall and winter colors. I was not as uncomfortable as I usually am with being the center of attention, and I sort of went with the flow of the evening as I have learned to do in life in general.

Only If

There were many well wishes and "Good for you for going for your dream." MJ never neglected to tell them I sold or gave away all I own before I even had an offer on the house, and am moving to Maui without even a job and have a place to stay for only a month. I was getting the feeling that I just might have done a shocking thing in most people's minds. It just seemed like a crystal clear decision to me.

It was a great evening and the last time we all got together. Pals, friends, buddies, dinner partners, brunch goers, someone to laugh with, to cry with and watch the Packers with, keepers of memories and secrets, and this the last of our heartfelt moments and mutual admirations shared just one more time.

My tickets for my personal adventure in paradise arrived that Saturday, and I had a pseudo-fight with Wendy to take possession from the FedEx man. Wendy was planning on stealing my tickets! She threatened the Fed Ex man that she would steal them from me so she could go instead, and I could stay and run her 70-plus children daycare center and look after her two boys until she returned. I think NOT!

Those last six days before departure were action-packed. I would leave Wendy's home in Green Bay at 8:00 a.m. and arrive back home at 9:45 p.m. I spent one entire day in De Pere, Kaukauna, and Wrightstown. I had my final visits and one more training opportunity with my replacements for four of my clients.

I stopped in Wrightstown to bid farewell to my neighbors, Judy and Eileen, and gave them a gold and crystal ornament to hang in their kitchen windows. They were just like the ones I gave to all my family and Hat Ladies. Naturally, my old home was just two doors away and I had to sneak a peek. The screens on the garage were packed away for the winter. The new owner had trimmed back the weigela as I had recommended. The dead flowers had been cleaned up, and I saw several piles of soil in the back. She was filling in the area by the back where the house had settled over the fourteen years. The only project I did not get done. I was glad the house was becoming her home.

The last weekend before I flew out I spent at my Aunt Sadie's in Iron Mountain, Michigan. The prime rib at T & T Supper Club was great, as usual. We have never found a better prime rib, and believe me, we have tried. The weather was cold as one would expect for Northern Michigan, but we had to have one more cup of coffee on the deck; one more night chatting on the love seat and davenport with afghans to stave off the chill of the night; one more night just hours before the dream she shared with me was about to come true.

It was wonderful being with family again, but oh so hard to say goodbye for the last time. Even though Sadie is my aunt, she has been like a sister to me all these years. I needed a friend when my mother died in 1959. She took on that role for me. She is my confidant, keeper of my memories. She has been so supportive; more than a family member needs to be, more like a true friend who loves me unconditionally.

I had thoughts of not moving to Hawaii more than once over the past months. My dad's cancer came back again in July after our surprise reunion. It did not look too good this time. He wanted all his children to live their lives and requested we not let what happened in his life to keep us from moving forward. And so I decided to go ahead with my plans.

On August 24, I drove to Iron Mountain, Michigan, to be with my aunt. She had called me earlier in the week to tell me Uncle Bob was in the hospital receiving dialysis and was not responding well to the treatments.

Only If

That Saturday night, we had a delayed birthday party for their daughter, Jody, in Uncle Bob's hospital room. It was such a heart-warming experience. All their children and grandchildren were there and I was honored to be there with them. The Packers were on the television for a pre-season football game, and we were all Packer fans and would not let a little hospital room spoil our fun.

Sadie made a thermos of coffee for the evening. We had plates, utensils and coffee cups. Jody and Glen had the cake. Cindy and Du, and Shawn and Ryan were there to watch the Packer game along with Bob, and we all chatted back and forth. We ended the evening with cake and coffee. As 9 p.m. grew near, one by one we all went to Bob to say goodnight and give him a kiss. He responded with a smile and a thumbs-up sign. It had been a lovely and loving evening.

Jody had been spending most nights at Bob's side. He was as my father was, and felt better with a family member spending the night when in the hospital. When Dad or Bob awoke in the middle of the night from a drug-induced dream, it was a comfort for them to have a familiar touch and loving face nearby.

Since it was Jody's birthday, his son Bobby offered to spend that night with his dad. At 6:30 Sunday morning, Bobby called Aunt Sadie to say that Bob had just passed away in his sleep. He was gone. We had one last night with him as a family. Now life was about to change for Sadie, too.

After we visited Bob one last time in the hospital, Sadie and I walked the grounds. Could I now leave her in her time of need? It took a few days to resolve that question in my heart. But Sadie had all her family within miles of her and I was over two hours away. They would be there for her on a day-to-day basis. I decided to be there for me this time and go ahead with my plans to move. My gift to Sadie's family would be my words at Bob's graveside.

I just realized the Saturday I received my tickets to Hawaii was the 20th. I received my tickets just seven months and one day after I made my decision to go after my dream and move to Hawaii. I would leave Green Bay at 9:00 a.m. and fly directly to Oahu from Minneapolis and arrive on Maui about 6:52 p.m. Tuesday, October 30. It was the second full moon in October. So my dream came true, "once in a blue moon."

When I had my corporation all those years ago, my corporate motto was "Dreams Are Realities That Are Yet To Be."

Guess I had it right even then.

Only If

Epilogue

I lived on Maui from October 2001 until June 2009, when I returned to Upper Michigan, a year after the death of my best friend, Aunt Sadie. I lost another great friend, Sheila, in 2011 to cancer. Both of their deaths made me realize just how short life is. My dad passed away on July 1, 2002.

I so loved my home and spiritual life on Maui that I decided to move back on April 1, 2013, and continue to live my dream, find my bliss, and live my passion. I used the internet to continue to work with the bookkeeping clients I had taken with me when I moved to Michigan and back to Maui.

Since my return to Maui, I found my current book editing team and have been working on finally getting this book completed. This all started in 2005 when I edited many letters I had written to my friend, Joyce, who moved to England in 1997. We made a deal to send emails twice a week. From these letters I found a lot of the details in this book.

My first editor read these letters and asked if she could pass them on to two other editors. I was teaching her QuickBooks and she could "hear me speaking" when she read my letters. She wanted a second opinion. They all loved the story of me making the decision on March 19, 2001, but thought a longer book would sell better.

Once I got several more chapters together, my first editor wanted more details of my personal life. It was very trying and I managed only three scant pages. I could not understand why anyone would find my upbringing of interest and stopped working on the book. We all have loss, why would mine be of interest? I had always kept all my secrets close to my heart.

Encouraged again by my current editors, I opened my mind and soul to face my past issues, perhaps for the best and final time. I hope you have enjoyed my journey. I have learned many lessons along this path - sometimes over and over again. I hope one or two may be of interest to you or someone you love as well.

Dream big! Set a goal with an end date – that is a dream with a deadline. I learned to face my unsolved issues – some issues I never knew I even had. Find your centering point or inner peace; find your bliss or your passion. Release any fears you have and find courage to make the life for you that you want.

Remember no matter where you go, what job you do, your constant companions are your thoughts, words and actions. Only a change in your choices, thoughts and attitude can lighten those burdens.

How do you eat an elephant? One bite at a time. And so it is with life. One bite, one action, one step at a time.

Here is a poem I fell in love with about 1988. I had it on a scrap of paper in my files and looked at it over the years. I had searched for it on the internet, but found it just this year.

Only If

A Quote by Gail Brook Burket on courage, strength, and paths

I do not ask to walk smooth paths
    Nor bear an easy load, I pray for strength and fortitude
        To climb the rock strewn road.
Give me such courage I can scale
    The hardest peaks alone
        And transform every stumbling block
            Into a stepping stone.

Thank you, Gail, for your inspiration.

Linda Lee Pope
June 15, 2014

Resources

I have learned many things through the years. It is hard to state what thoughts are mine and what I have absorbed from my mentors and made them part of the changes I made in my life – they became the new and improved me. I thank them one and all.

There have been many, many mentors in my life. They range from family and friends to seminar leaders and their wisdoms. After my divorce in 1977, a friend gave me a new book by Shakti Gawain called *Creative Visualization*, a concept I had never heard of and worked for years to master.

I was given a book after my daughter's death in 1984. The book was *Gifts from the Sea* by Anne Morrow Lindberg. She, too, had lost a child in 1932. It gave me peace and comfort, and taught me how to write stories about my life's experiences.

They had a piece of property on Maui next to the Seven Scared Pools of 'Ohe'o. I went there on my visit to Maui in 1986. I touched the desk she wrote at; I looked out the window she did as she wrote; I could see the steps she used to walk down to the sea.

In the late 1970s, I started searching for things in life I did not know about and put in my life to learn and grow. I began with works from motivational speakers like Zig Zigler, Jim Rohn, Joseph Campbell and Dr. Wayne Dyer.

Only If

I read many books over the years, some I found at the local library. I wanted to list the books and audios that I found helpful to me:

John Bradshaw

Bradshaw On the Family: ten-part series, 1985
Healing the Shame that Binds You: one-hour program, 1987
Adult Children Of Dysfunctional Families: two-hour program, 1988
Bradshaw On Homecoming: ten-part series, 1990
Bradshaw On: Family Secrets: six-part series, 1995

Dan Millman

Way of the Peaceful Warrior
Sacred Journey
Journeys of Socrates
Everyday Enlightenment
No Ordinary Moments ** My favorite!
Laws of Spirit

James Redfield

The Celestine Prophecy: An Adventure by James Redfield
The Tenth Insight: Holding The Vision by James Redfield
Secret of Shambhala: In Search of the Eleventh Insight
The Twelfth Insight: The Hour of Decision

Acknowledgements

I lost my mother at the age of thirteen. I turned to the library, audio tapes and books to learn those things a mom can teach you through life experiences. Some mentors are mentioned in the Resource section. Most items were free to teach me. I learned about cooking from PBS and Julia Child. As my income grew, I purchased books to read and reread, learning new things with each reading.

I had many friends and mentors along the way who accepted me for what I was and the woman I would become thanks to their love and acceptance. To Wendy, Doris, Judy. Eileen and the Hat Ladies in and around Green Bay, Wisconsin. To my Aunt Sadie, who was my best friend and mentor the first sixty years of my life until her death. I lived with my grandparents for nearly six years, and Goodman, Wisconsin, became my adopted home town, nestled in the north woods of Wisconsin. The north woods and nature became the way I connected to my God and spirituality, and rediscovered on Maui.

Many of my friends were from Maui after my move here in 2001; mostly clients who turned into friends, like Barb, my webmaster, Maggi, Michele, Kehau, Agnes and Martha were just a few.

To Joyce, living in England since 1997, and Sheila from Wausau, Wisconsin, who knew all my secrets now revealed in this book. We only lived in the same towns for a few years, but kept in contact with long letters and weekend phone calls since 1988 and 1977, respectively. Those two were my adopted sisters.

Only If

To Anne and Bonnie, my two primary book editors. Anne helped me turn 167 letters to Joyce into a book and encouraged me to write about my personal life. Bonnie became my editor in 2014 and encouraged me to face my past and write about my personal life experiences that are now the first few chapters. I have learned those things that offer the most resistance are things we need to face, honor and place it in the past where they belong. Thank you also to Mike and Amy at M&B Global Solutions, who looked through my manuscript with a fine-toothed comb to complete the final editing.

And to my son, Michael, and sisters, Leeanna, Louse, Leslie and Lisa. The loss of our mother in 1959 put a big hole in our life. It took years and years to fill in the holes and learn what we needed to learn to survive life's trials. And to our father, who lost the love of his life in 1959 and was left alone to raise six children from 13 years to three weeks of age—without a sitter or nanny. Somehow we survived and learned to thrive.

Thank you, one all, for the woman I am today.

Only If

About the Author

Linda Lee Pope is Wisconsin born and raised. In October of 2001, she fulfilled a dream by moving to the Hawaiian island of Maui at the age of 56.

In August of 1959 at the age of thirteen, she was thrust into a new role with the unexpected death of her mother. Linda was the oldest of six children as young as three weeks in age.

A new show came on television in black and white two months after her mother's passing. It was *Adventures in Paradise*. Once a week, Linda would escape her world for an hour and travel the South Sea Islands with the show's main character, Captain Adam Troy.

The show planted the seeds for a dream that stayed with Linda for forty years, to live her own life in tropical paradise. Through good times and bad, she kept a goal to keep her company, to escape, and to dream.